W9-CEA-319

British Columbia

British Columbia

AN ILLUSTRATED HISTORY

Geoffrey Molyneux

Published by:
Polestar Press Ltd.
P.O. Box 69382, Station K
Vancouver, B.C.
V5K 4W6

Distributed by:
Raincoast Book Distribution Ltd.
112 East Third Avenue
Vancouver, B.C.
V5T 1C8

This book has been published with the financial assistance
of the Canada Council and the
British Columbia Cultural Services Branch

Book design and cover art by Jim Brennan
Maps by Jim Brennan
Newspaper reproductions by Sandra Robinson
Production by Michelle Benjamin
Printed in Canada

Canadian Cataloguing in Publication Data

Molyneux, Geoffrey.
British Columbia

Includes bibliographical references and index.
ISBN 0-919591-18-3

1. British Columbia—History. I. Title.
FC3811.M64 1992 971.1 C92-091296-6
F1087.M64 1992

CONTENTS

PREFACE

British Columbia: An Illustrated History contains all the usual ingredients of a history. There are stories about women, men and children, politics, business, the land and the sea. There's a lot of skullduggery, and a little sacrifice. You'll also find photographs, maps, graphics, anecdotes and intriguing snippets that add to your understanding and, we hope, entertainment.

Where does it all come from? Books, magazines, newspapers, television and radio programs, and gossip. All treated with a pinch of common sense. This book is closer to good journalism than to academic history.

At the end of each chapter is a fanciful look at a moment in time—a moment that sums up the events and changes described in the text. These epiphanies are mixtures of fact and fiction based, mostly, on contemporary accounts and reports.

WINDS OF CHANGE
10,000 Years Ago to 1858

NATIVE PEOPLE BUILD COMPLEX SOCIETY

EUROPEANS ARRIVE TO EXPLORE, EXPLOIT, TRADE AND CONQUER

FUR TRADE ON LAND AND SEA

GOLD BRINGS THREAT OF INVASION

AROUND THE WORLD
EUROPE, CHINA, RUSSIA — 450,000 YEARS AGO Arrival of Homo Sapiens
GREECE — 2,500 YEARS AGO Sparta Dominates Grecian City States
PARIS — 1778 Mozart Scores Minor Success with Paris Symphony, No. 31

*POPULATION — 1770	
Native People	est. 90,000
1850	
Native People	est. 60,000 (99%)
Europeans	est. 600 (1%)

*ETHNIC ORIGIN

Who were the first people to live in what we call British Columbia? Where did they come from and what kind of people were they?

No-one knows the precise answers to these questions but most experts agree that the first people to live in Canada arrived some time during the last Ice Age—between 80,000 and 12,000 years ago. It seems that these first migrants came from Asia over a strip of land now covered by the Bering Sea. Through a corridor between the ice masses (it ran south-south east along the east side of what are now the Rockies), they slowly moved to what is now the Midwest of the United States. As the ice receded, they migrated north. Around 11,000 years ago there were people living in parts of what is now British Columbia.

We know this because archaeologists digging in a pit near Fort St. John have found stone tools, weapons and carved bison bones which they say are 11,000 years old. The

The life of the native peoples of the coast—the Haida, Tsimshian, Bella Coola, Kwakiutl, Nootka and Coast Salish—seems to have changed when the sea level stopped fluctuating around 5,000 years ago. As sea shores and river deltas developed, fish and shellfish became easier to catch and preserve for later use. Now people had time for doing more than just gathering food—such as building and decorating homes, weaving, making boats of cedar, and tools and weapons of bone and stone. Life was harder for the people of the Interior—the Sekani, Slave, Beaver, Carrier, Chilcotin, Shuswap, Tahltan, Kaska, Thompson, Lillooet, Okanagan and Kootenay. Food was harder to get and the climate harsher.

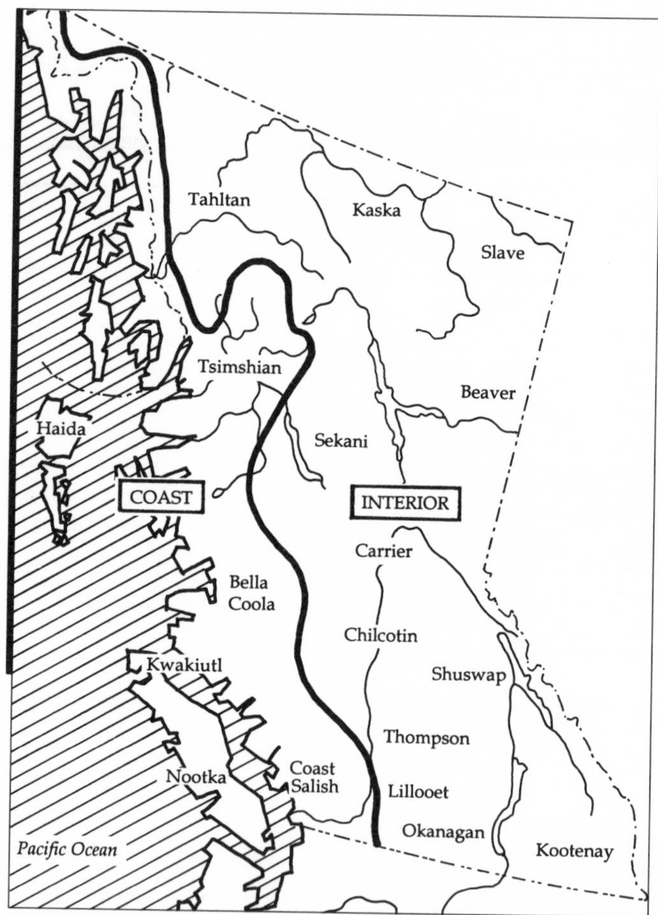

people who left these pieces of evidence lived in tents or caves and hunted bison and other animals. It seems safe to assume that similar bands of hunters and their families were roaming the uplands of central British Columbia around that time. About 7,000 years ago, these people of the Interior began to move into the river valleys and fish for salmon. They started to build homes excavated into the ground and to use tools archaeologists call micro-blades—primitive razor blades chipped from rock by craftsmen.

The Pacific coast of B.C. does not fit neatly into this pattern, however. The people who lived on the coast and along the rivers close to the sea seem to have had other roots. They used tools different from those used in the

Interior. Perhaps they were descendants of a group which came over the Bering bridge much later; perhaps they came south by sea. There is general agreement that people have been living on the coast for more than 9,000 years. We know this from diggings at Namu, on the mainland coast just north of Vancouver Island, and at Lawn Point, on Graham Island in the Queen Charlottes.

The life led by these coastal people changed rapidly when the sea-level stopped fluctuating 5,000 to 6,000 years ago. The coastline became permanent, and river deltas and tidal flats developed. Fish and shellfish became much easier to catch and harvest; settlements grew and population increased. Now fish could be stored by drying or smoking on the shore and this left time for activities other than gathering food. Men and women developed the skills and tools to build homes, boats, make nets, weave clothes and make harpoons, fishhooks, knives and weapons from bone and stone. Trade routes opened to the Interior, and exotic objects such as personal jewellery and decorated housewares, as well as mundane products like eulachan oil, were exchanged for hides and food.

Around 2,500 years ago, the people in the Fraser delta, the central mainland coast, northern Vancouver Island, and in the Queen Charlottes and Prince Rupert areas had developed a sophisticated social system with elaborate

Detail from An Inside view of the Natives Habitation—*a Nootka woman weaving bark cloth, part of a 1778 drawing by John Webber, an artist who sailed with Cook.*

The leader of the most powerful group in Nootka Sound always took the name of Maquinna. He greeted Cook and the Spanish and traded with the British and American fur traders. The rascally John Meares, a British Captain, claimed that in Spring, 1788 Maquinna gave him land at Nootka on which he built a trading post. After being insulted in 1803 by the captain of the Boston, *Maquinna and his men massacred the captain and his crew and took two men captive. They lived with Maquinna as his slaves until they were freed in 1805.*

rituals, a spiritual life and an artistic tradition. Their economic system, perfectly suited to their environment, supplied them with food, clothes, homes and weapons. Archaeological diggings in the Fraser Valley, Cache Creek, Kamloops and Crowsnest Pass areas show communities leading similar but probably less elaborate lives.

The Nootka people of northern Vancouver Island were the first in B.C. to spend some time with Europeans. These European explorers and traders came from societies eager to learn about new worlds, and so they wrote books and reports and drew sketches about the people they met, people who seemed strange and exotic. As a result, we know more about the life led by the Nootka in the late eighteenth century than about other groups.

The Nootka seem to have cultivated few plants, but their supply of meat was abundant: fish, shellfish, deer, elk, bear, goat, seals, porpoises and whales were all part of their diet.

The men built the homes from large planks and posts, burned out the insides of large trees to build canoes, and developed tools of stone and bone to split and fashion the cedar they found around them. While the men fished and hunted, the women gathered shellfish, prepared and preserved the food, and wove clothes from cedar bark. They also made the nets for fishing and the mats for the communal homes.

Family groups consisted of people related by ancestry, passed on by either male or female lines, and they lived together in large homes. Most property, such as land, homes or fishing sites, belonged to one of these groups or their leader. They used captives taken in battle or raids as slaves.

The lot of children and women was not happy. Children were sometimes sold and enslaved. Women had virtually no choice in marriage and were expected to be monogamous. But women were not necessarily submissive and weak. Some early traders reported that the men were abused and beaten by the women for failing to get a good price for skins. Female slaves and lower-class women were used as drudges, prostitutes for visitors (such as the Europeans), or bed partners.

The winds and tides that brought these Pacific coast

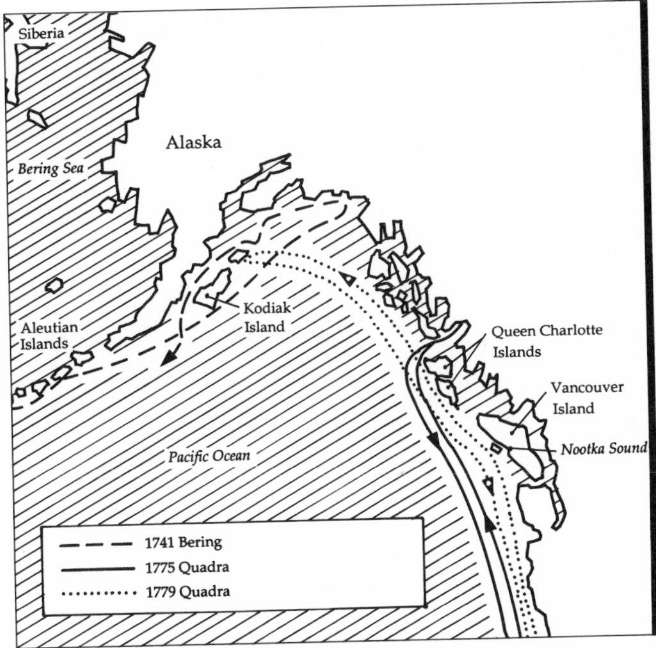

Vitus Bering, a Dane working for the Russians, confirmed in 1729 that a broad stretch of water—now the Bering Strait—separated Asia and America. He explored the American North Pacific coast in 1740-41 to a latitude of 55° N. Bering died of scurvy during the voyage.

The Spanish 82-foot frigate Santiago, *commanded by Juan Hernandez, sailed from Mexico, reached the Queen Charlottes and traded with the Haida in 1774. In 1775, the Spanish sailed north again. This time the* Santiago *was accompanied by the* Sonora, *commanded by Juan de la Bodega y Quadra (who negotiated with Captain George Vancouver 17 years later). Quadra reached 57° N. Quadra sailed north again as a member of the 1779 expedition. He reached 60° N.*

people their food and warm, wet climate also brought massive changes. Europeans, driven by the desire for wealth, power, knowledge and the perceived need to bring the salvation of the Church to unfortunate natives, sailed into the Pacific in the early sixteenth century. (Some native peoples told the Europeans of strange ships wrecked on the coast—probably Japanese—but times and places were vague.)

It was not until the middle of the 18th century that serious exploration began. First came the Spanish, sailing north from Mexico, and the Russians from their frigid northeastern ports. Then, in 1774, the Spanish met the Haida off the Queen Charlottes and later, driven south by storms, sought shelter in what we now call Nootka Sound.

Two years later, on July 12, 1776, Captain James Cook sailed from Plymouth in the west of England in the 420-ton *Resolution*, ahead of his other ship, *Discovery*. In early 1778 he was in the north Pacific and came upon some islands he named for his powerful patron, the fourth Earl of Sandwich—now the Hawaiian islands. Cook was riding a crest of fame after two successful voyages of explora-

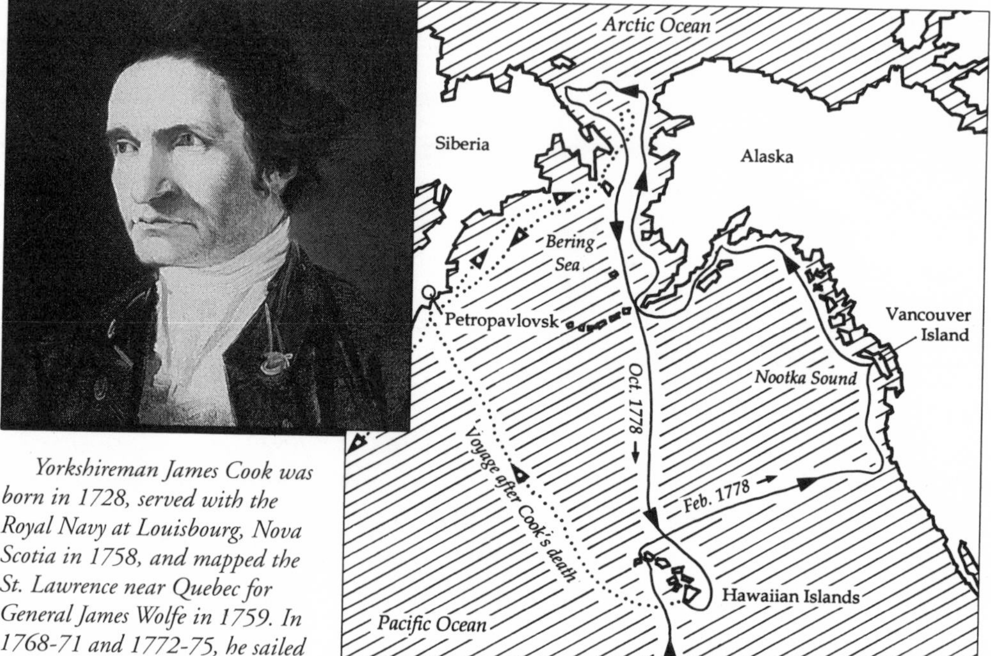

Yorkshireman James Cook was born in 1728, served with the Royal Navy at Louisbourg, Nova Scotia in 1758, and mapped the St. Lawrence near Quebec for General James Wolfe in 1759. In 1768-71 and 1772-75, he sailed around the world, exploring and mapping parts of Australia, New Zealand, Antarctica and the islands of the South Pacific. In 1776 he set out to find the Northwest Passage from the Pacific but was turned back two years later by ice in the Bering Strait. Bad weather dogged Cook's ships when he reached the Pacific Northwest coast on March 7, 1778, and headed north. He may be excused, then, for missing the mouth of the Columbia and the Strait of Juan de Fuca, both on his course. Captain George Vancouver, 14 years later, did little better. He missed the Columbia and had no excuses. Cook was killed in a squabble on the Sandwich Islands (Hawaii) February 14, 1779.

tion to Australia, New Zealand, the south Pacific and Antarctica. This time his orders from the Admiralty told him to look for the Northwest passage which had eluded explorers searching from the Atlantic side.

On February 2, 1778, Cook left Hawaii, beating before the wind towards the coast that was the last stretch of land in the world's temperate zones still unexplored by Europeans. On March 7, using a new chronometer—an accurate watch that helped him determine exact longitude—and the other navigational aids provided by the Admiralty (aids only recently supplanted by radar and satellite navigation), *Resolution* and *Discovery* came to the coast of the Pacific Northwest at 44 degrees 33 minutes north latitude—central Oregon. Gales forced Cook and the *Resolution's* master and navigator, William Bligh, to sail up the uncharted coast well out to sea for three weeks, even though they were running short of water and needed to repair *Resolution's* masts. As a result, they missed the mouth of the Columbia River and the Strait of Juan de Fuca. At four in the afternoon on March 29, through a break in the weather, the ships sighted a gap in the coastline and edged their way into the inlet we now call Friendly Cove, in Nootka Sound.

Cook and his ships stayed in Nootka until April 26. His men set up an observatory, explored the inlet, repaired their rotting masts, and traded knick-knacks and pieces of metal—anything from nails to pewter plates—for sea otter furs. Everyone got on well together but the seeds of decay had been sown: disease and a foreign set of values were to disrupt a society that had evolved over thousands of years.

Cook sailed north from Nootka to start the search for the Northwest Passage. When his men next touched land—in Russian territory—they found that the furs they had bought for plates or buttons were worth hundreds of pounds. News of the fortunes to be made on the Pacific Northwest coast reached the Far East, England and Europe, and by the mid-1780s other ships were trading for sea otter furs. One of these, sailing under the Austrian flag to avoid British licensing laws, was commanded by Charles Barkley. He brought along his seventeen-year-old, red-haired bride Frances—the first white woman to visit British Columbia.

All this activity revived Spanish interest in Nootka, and in May 1789 the Spanish started to build a fort close to the shore. To assert their sovereignty over the area, they captured some of the men working for John Meares, a renegade British Captain and trader, who claimed that, a year before, Nootka Chief Maquinna had granted him land and the right to build a trading post. Meares went to England, raved about the treachery and arrogance of the Spanish, and persuaded the British government to devote two million pounds for war with Spain. But diplomacy won the day. After all, the Revolution in France, just across the Channel, was bigger stuff than events in a tiny inlet thousands of miles away. Britain and Spain signed the Nootka Convention in October 1790 and Spain seemed to have dropped its claim to sovereignty over the Pacific

Captain George Vancouver served with Captain Cook as a 15-year-old midshipman on his great 1772-75 voyage and also served on his expedition to the Pacific Northwest in 1776-79. In April 1792, Vancouver was back in the Pacific Northwest, charged with settling the Nootka incident and with mapping the coast leading to the Northwest Passage. Before returning to England, he mapped Puget Sound, Georgia Strait, Burrard Inlet and Vancouver Island. Vancouver died May 12, 1798.

Juan Francisco de la Bodega y Quadra was born in Lima, Peru in 1743. From 1775 to 1779 he commanded Spanish Navy ships exploring the Pacific Northwest coast and in 1789 was in charge of the naval station at San Blas, Mexico. In 1792 Quadra was in command of the Spanish settlement at Nootka, where he met Captain Vancouver to try to settle the Anglo-Spanish dispute over sovereignty of the area. Quadra died in 1793.

Northwest. Meares got his men back.

This was still unknown territory and both Britain and Spain decided to do more exploring and to name envoys who could meet and settle the dispute. Spain named Don Juan Francisco de la Bodega y Quadra; Britain assigned Captain George Vancouver, who had sailed to Nootka with Cook 14 years before. Both eminently reasonable fellows, Quadra and Vancouver co-operated in mapping the coastline and, after meeting at Nootka, agreed to disagree and let their governments work things out. After two years of exploration and mapping, Vancouver left for home; a revised Nootka Convention was signed the same year. Spain effectively dropped claims to the Pacific Northwest. From now on it was a tussle between Britain and the new United States, with Russia playing a minor, spoiling role.

While Yankee fur traders and Spanish and British navy officers were jostling for position on the coast, the great land explorers were exploring the Interior for the British-controlled fur trade. The North West Company, a loosely-knit group of fur traders competing with the Hudson's Bay Company, sent three men—Alexander Mackenzie, Simon Fraser and David Thompson—to find new sources of furs, open trading posts and find routes to the Pacific.

Mackenzie failed on his first try to reach the Pacific overland and ended up on the bleak Arctic shoreline. He went back to England, learned surveying and astronomy, and tried again. On July 22, 1793, after following native trails and listening to the advice of helpful native men and women, he reached the Pacific Ocean near Bella Coola. But the native trails he followed hardly made a good route for the fur trade.

Then it was Simon Fraser's turn. In 1775 the Spanish had seen the mouth of a massive river flowing into the Pacific around 46°N latitude. Both Cook and Vancouver had sailed past the mouth without noticing it. Then, in 1792 American fur trader Robert Gray, had sailed into the

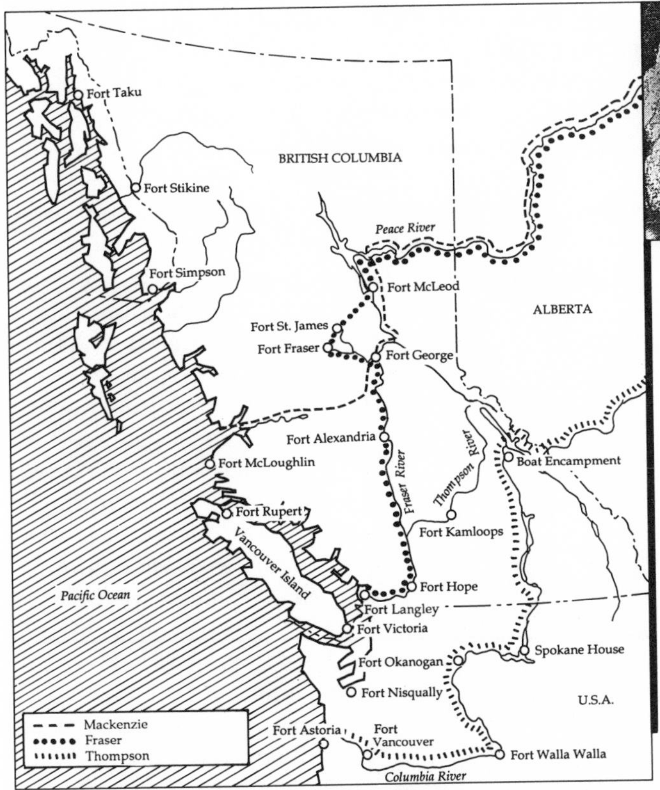

Routes and forts of the fur traders: the fur-trader explorers looked for land and water routes, a good supply of furs and sites for settlements—often optimistically called forts.

Alexander Mackenzie reached the Pacific overland while Vancouver's men were still mapping the coast. Mackenzie created the first graffiti on the Pacific coast. On a rock at Bella Coola he wrote in grease coloured with vermilion: "Alex Mackenzie, from Canada by land, 22d July, 1793."

river and named it for his ship, the *Columbia.* In 1805, more Americans—Meriwether Lewis and William Clark—leading a government-sponsored expedition, reached the mouth of the Columbia and planted the United States flag. Fraser's task, then: to find a route through New Caledonia (central B.C.) to the mouth of the Columbia. In the spring of 1808 he canoed down streams and torrents, hacked his way through the bush, clung to cliffs and at last sailed into the estuary of what was later called the Fraser River. But the native people of the estuary, the Musqueam, were none too friendly and, after taking his astronomical readings, Fraser realized that he had not found the Columbia.

David Thompson did find a route to the Columbia through the Kootenays in southeastern B.C. But he took so long to get from Lake Windermere that by the time he reached the Columbia in July 1811, he found the Americans of John Jacob Astor's company already there, building their trading post called Fort Astoria.

Despite the squabbles between the U.S. and Britain over land around the mouth of the Columbia, the fur trade of New Caledonia prospered. The North West Company, which merged with the Hudson's Bay Company in 1821, opened new trading posts—optimistically called forts—on the rivers, lakes and trails of the Interior.

Although the Americans had sold their post on the Columbia to the Canadian company, political uncertainty encouraged the Hudson's Bay Company to seek a post further north, with access to the Pacific and in land that had never been claimed by the increasingly aggressive American administration in Washington.

The padle steamer Beaver—*which served Pacific ports for nearly 60 years—lies in ruins off Prospect Point, Stanley Park, Vancouver. She ran aground July 26, 1889. Contemporary accounts imply that her crew had been celebrating none too wisely before her last trip.*

Fort Langley was built in 1827, 20 miles up the Fraser. It soon became a new kind of trading post: a farm and salmon-processing plant as well as warehouse and strong point. Vegetables, grain and fish products were shipped first to other company posts and then to other countries. A steamship, the *Beaver*, sailed from a Thames shipyard around the Horn to the Columbia in 1836 and began a coastal service picking up furs and delivering supplies.

In 1842, Chief Factor James Douglas sailed up from the Columbia and picked a site at the tip of Vancouver Island for another Hudson's Bay Company post. Construction began in the spring of 1843 with the help of the Songhee people who were paid in blankets. The new post, protected by a two-story bastion with a nine-pounder gun, became Fort Victoria. Soon the fields around Fort Victoria were being farmed. Dairy cows were imported from the U.S. and grain and vegetables were produced to feed Fort Victoria's population and for sale to Russian fur traders on the northern coast.

As Fort Victoria was being built, the first large wave of settlers came into Oregon Territory, and the campaign in the U.S. to control the Northwest up to 54°40 minutes north—the border with Russia—gained speed. On June 15, 1846, Britain and the United States split their differences over the border and signed the Treaty of Washington. It established the 49th parallel as the border; Britain gave up its claim to what is now Washington State and part of Oregon, and the U.S. gave up the northern border of 54/40.

James Douglas was born in British Guiana in 1803, the son of a Scotsman and a Creole woman. He was educated in Scotland and joined the North West Company in 1819. He served as a fur trader, joined the Hudson's Bay Company in the merger of 1821, and in 1828 married Amelia Connolly, the 16-year-old daughter of Chief Factor Connolly and a native woman. Douglas was intelligent, forceful and daring, and quickly rose to the rank of Chief Factor at Fort Vancouver in what is now Oregon. Douglas built Fort Victoria in 1843 and ran the Hudson's Bay Company's fiefdom from there. He became governor of Vancouver Island in 1851 and of British Columbia in 1858. Douglas retired in 1864.

Although they still had rights to trapping and trade below the new border, the Hudson's Bay Company decided to transfer its operations to Fort Victoria. In the spring of 1849, James Douglas brought his wife and daughters there and took charge of the company on the Island and in the Interior. Douglas's wife, Amelia, was the daughter of a company fur trader and his Cree wife. She was typical of the many women of full or half-Indian blood who lived with or were married to the Scots, Orkney, Shetland and English men who worked for the company. Their daughters, educated and often brought up like English misses, married the single young men who came to the Island to farm or help run the company.

As Douglas was moving in, the Colonial Office in Westminster made Vancouver Island a crown colony and leased it to the Hudson's Bay Company for ten years. One of Douglas' duties, it was ordered, was to encourage settlement by men and women of English stock. This, the

Amelia Connolly (centre, surrounded by family) was typical of the native and half-breed women who bore and cared for the children of the fur traders. She was born in 1812 to William Connolly of the North West Company, and Suzanne, the daughter of a Cree chief. James Douglas married her on April 27, 1828. Soon afterwards, the 16-year-old Amelia saved Douglas's life when he was captured by members of the Stuart band. Two years later, Douglas was transferred to Fort Vancouver. Amelia was pregnant and so her father took her to Douglas with the fur brigade a few months later. Douglas was upset when she arrived for he was proud of her fair skin, auburn hair and grey eyes and the long journey had given her a tan. Amelia Douglas had 13 children. Five were still alive when she joined her husband at Fort Victoria in 1849; one baby died but two more were born in Victoria, the last when she was 42 years old. Because of her mixed blood, Amelia Douglas was scorned by the racist and snobbish women of Victoria society.

Colonial Office believed, was the only peaceful way to keep the pushy Americans out. Young Englishmen were encouraged to come to the island to farm. Sawmills started working to produce lumber for homes and farms, and for export to Hawaii and San Francisco. Coal mines were dug at Fort Rupert on the northern tip of the island in 1849 and at Nanaimo in 1852. A school for girls was opened in 1849, and in 1850 the first colonial governor arrived.

Richard Blanshard stepped off a Royal Navy ship on March 9, 1850. No home was ready for him and he had no salary or official funds. Seven months later he wrote his resignation letter to the Colonial Office but had to wait ten months before a ship brought him a letter saying that he was relieved of his office. Douglas, the real governor all along, took over officially. Blanshard spent most of his waiting time writing letters complaining that Douglas was doing little to encourage settlement. By 1854 there were only 250 people living in the farms around Victoria—mostly on land that had been bought by Douglas from the native people in land settlements

Then, on Sunday, April 25, 1858, the people of Victoria came out of church to find the paddlesteamer *Commodore* had just docked from San Francisco with 450 miners eager to start looking for gold.

Aboard *Resolution*

March 28, 1778

It's four o'clock in the afternoon and most of the officers and men on the deck of the *Resolution*, a converted North Sea collier, are on the starboard rail. They're looking for the first signs of land as their ship inches north along the North Pacific coast.

Resolution's master, William Bligh, has just watched the men reef the topsails to get ready for the evening gales which have plagued their lives since they left the Sandwich Islands three weeks ago. Every now and then the men can see *Resolution's* sister ship, *Discovery*, through the spray well astern. Both ships are keeping well out to sea, for this is an unknown coastline and the winds make manoeuvring well-nigh impossible.

Cook's chronometer—he called it a watch—from his second and third voyages. It was made by Larcum Kendall in 1769, named K1, and was a copy of the first chronometer made by inventor John Harrison. After Cook's ships returned to England, K1 was used in the first surveys of New South Wales.

The officers make room. *Resolution's* commander has come on deck from his cabin.

"Take care," Bligh says softly to young George Vancouver. "Guard your tongue and agree with every word he utters. He's in one of his foul moods. Surgeon Samwell says his guts are griping again. He'll be on the lookout for anything wrong."

Vancouver looks at Captain Cook.

"But he's always been a charmer. Very just. He looks after his men's health, uses the lash rarely...why the change?"

Bligh looks at Vancouver, then holds his hands on his belly. Cook pushes Vancouver out of his way and confronts Bligh.

"Mr. Bligh. If you know what's good for you, you had better find us some snug cove—and fast—or you'll be Master no longer."

Bligh, never at a loss for words or courage, starts to reply, but Cook carries on.

"We need to fill up our fresh-water barrels and get some fresh food."

A stronger gust hits the ship, and Cook looks up at the foremast.

"And you know as well as I that we have to repair the rotten foremast those dolts at Deptford put in this ship. And my cabin leaks. Some of the men are sleeping in water. The first thing I'll do when we reach the Downs is get to Deptford and tell those buffoons how they nearly wrecked my ship."

Bligh points out to his commander that the dockyard was busy preparing men-of-war for the battle with the rebellious colonists in North America, and so was short of time and materials.

Model of a ship similar to Cook's: below decks every inch of space is crammed with stores, with little room for the officers and other crew.

Cook snorts. "You can always find some excuse, Mister Bligh. I hope you have one ready to explain your failure to find us a place to escape these winds. You have the best watches, sextants, quadrants, clocks and telescopes the Admiralty could buy from the instrument-makers in London. When I started to learn the navigator's art we had to make do with half of the instruments you have on this ship. What's the use of all those mathematicians, all those inventors, coal miners, furnacemen and craftsmen working hard if you can't find your way to a safe shelter?"

Cook turns away and gazes out at the sea. Bligh, a fine navigator with abundant confidence in his skill, smiles at Vancouver.

The 113 men on board—25 officers (including an artist, surgeon and astronomer), 15 Marines and 73 carpenters, artificers, blacksmiths and seamen—want to find land as eagerly as the captain.

With 113 men in a ship only 110 feet long, it's easy for tempers to run high. The air below decks crammed with supplies and equipment gets damp and smelly when the hatches are battened down. If Cook weren't such a stickler for cleanliness and sensible food on his ships, there'd be disease on board.

Below, in the tiny galley with its wood-fired stove, two seamen are helping the cook.

"What's this New Albion going to be like, then?"

The older of the two men measures out the ingredients for the evening meal—four ounces of dried peas to every quart of boiling water, with ten ounces of dehydrated soup—and stirs them in a cauldron. The other seaman scours a pot with sand.

"Can't be worse than here."

"At least we'll stand a chance of getting

some fresh food," he says."Anything to get away from these peas. Even when we cook them for hours, they're still as hard as shot for the marines' muskets."

"The salt pork and beef not to your liking, then?"

The young man grimaces.

"If it was calmer, we could catch some fish—or even a porpoise."

"Or a shark." Both men laugh.

"Shows you how the navy works. Remember the day Charlie Todd caught that shark? She had young'uns inside her and the officers got the tender babies and we had the tough old mother."

The seamen aren't the only ones looking forward to fresh food. The sheep and goats on board can sense the closeness of land. A stay in port means that the men will be ordered ashore to gather fresh grass, plants and vegetables for them.

Resolution, with *Discovery* trying hard to keep in hailing distance, sails on. There's a dirty, rainy evening ahead.

In Friendly Cove

March 28, 1778

It's late afternoon and the men and women of the Nootka people are at work close to their summer homes on the sea shore. They moved here from their inland homes about 30 days ago when the herring and spring salmon arrived off the coast.

The Nootka people spent most of the fall and winter in their homes on the banks of rivers and inlets where they could get shelter from the driving winds and rain. They lived on the fish they had preserved for the long winter, and on the deer, bears, rabbits and other animals they hunted in the forest. During the long winter nights, there were many ceremonies and feasts. Before they left for the coast, for example, they celebrated the return of a man who had been captured in a raid by another tribe and ransomed by the chief. The chief, his wives and children, invited guests, commoners—all seated according to rank—were served by slaves and enjoyed songs, speeches and performances by jesters and dancers in between courses.

The Nootka people started to move back towards the coast when they ran out of food. Moving house was not a difficult task—years ago they picked the sites for their homes and built frames there. When they arrive they only have to put up large planks to form the roof and walls.

A visitor from the Interior is staying with the Nootka people and is being shown how they catch fish and other seafood.

We're catching salmon this afternoon, he's told. We go out, one man in each canoe, and tie a trolling line baited with herring to our paddle. The catching part is easy for there are lots of salmon and the swishing of the paddle attracts them. We catch only enough spring salmon to eat today. We're not allowed to keep this kind of fish overnight.

What about other fish? the visitor asks.

Herring are caught by two or three men in a canoe using a nettle fibre net or a rake, his Nootka friend explains. This fish is eaten raw or broiled by the women over fir fires. Sometimes it's boiled in wooden boxes in water heated by hot stones. The women will clean and split the herring and dry them over fires of damp cedar.

It's a pity you spent so long in the house, the Nootka man tells the visitor. It's herring spawning time and you missed seeing how we get ready to collect the spawn. The slaves and the women spent this morning cutting boughs from trees. They set them in the sand at low water where the high tides will cover them in about 15 feet of water. When the boughs are coated with spawn, we'll drag them out, dry the eggs and store them in cedar boxes for the winter.

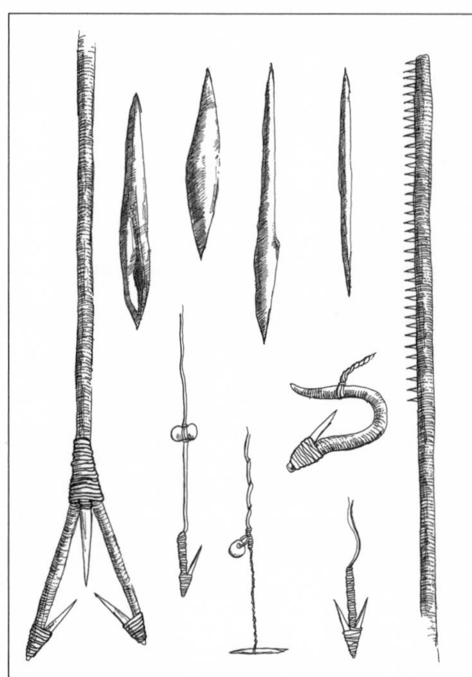

Fishing tools used by the Nootka people.

And if you stay through the summer you might see a whale hunt. As soon as the whales are spotted off the coast, we celebrate with dances and ceremonies. Then the chief will lead the whale hunt. His wife must go to bed and lie still while her husband is preparing to harpoon the whale. If she moves—even a little bit—the whale will move, too.

What's a harpoon? It's a long, special spear tipped with a razor-sharp mussel shell. We tie bladders to the harpoon with long twine and they slow the whale down and show us where it is.

The Nootka man and his guest go to watch some men unload their catches. Now's our chance to look inside a Nootka house.

It was built by placing thick fir trunks into the ground. Then they were then notched to hold planks of various sizes. A large round beam was set across these trunks as the main roof support. Big planks, overlapping each other, form the walls; more giant planks form the roof. Since they are not fastened to the main beam nor to any of the supports, they can be moved to let in light or allow smoke to escape. Other beams are supported by thick columns with human faces carved on them.

Around the inside of the house are boxes of various sizes, decorated with mouldings inlaid with animals' teeth. Some are still open and we can see that this is where the Nootka keep their capes, masks, and all kinds of ceremonial belongings. Along the walls are platforms with mats to be used as beds—each of them in a compartment separated from its neighbour by a low partition. Strings of dried fish and shellfish are strung from the beams. Hanging from hooks on the walls are bladders filled with oil.

The focal point of the house is an upright, oblong box—about the height of a man. Inside, a figure with a human face has been painted. It has long arms tipped with claws like an eagle, and feet like a bear. This is probably a prayer room.

And in the middle of the house—in the space between the sleeping compartments—are large fireplaces. Next to them are places where, we can see, fish and shellfish are cleaned and prepared for the evening meal.

Now the Nootka man comes back into he house and starts to rubs two sticks together to light a fire. When the fire is hot enough, he explains to his guest, large stones will be put into the middle. The women will pick out the stones with wooden tongs and put them into buckets of water with fish in them; this will boil the fish. When they are ready—the process sometimes has to be repeated a few times—the people of the house will be called in for the evening meal.

The *Resolution* and *Discovery* in Ship Cove, *from a 1778 painting by John Webber.*

CHOOSING CANADA 1858 to 1871

From Fort to Colony to Province

Miners and Settlers Open Up the Land

Disputes with U.S.A.

B.C. Delegates Receive Offer They Can't Refuse

AROUND THE WORLD
China — 1858 French and British troops force Emperor to allow Western traders
Germany — 1867 Karl Marx publishes first volume of *Das Kapital*
United States — 1863 Northern troops win decisive victory at Gettysburg

*POPULATION — 1871	
Native People	est. 25,000 (69%)
Europeans	8,576 (24%)
Asians	1,548 (4%)
Others	1,123 (3%)
Total	36,247

*ETHNIC ORIGIN

Men had been mining underground gold for centuries but it was a job for skilled workers and heavy equipment. Placer (free) gold, however, found in streams and near the surface, could be mined by almost anyone. In 1848 some free gold was found in Sutter's Creek in California. All was set for the first gold rush. The new telegraph and the new urban newspapers spread the news and the new steamships were ready to carry prospectors, miners and their helpers, suppliers and entertainers to the gold.

In 1851, free gold was found by natives in the Queen Charlotte Islands. Governor James Douglas kept the news secret and persuaded the Colonial Office in London to give him control of the Charlottes—an invasion by the aggressive, gold- and land-hungry Americans was to be avoided at all costs. The gold in the Charlottes fizzled out but in 1856 Victoria learned that natives, using spoons and pieces of pottery, were scooping gold from

Rugged country and rugged men: miners at the Seymour Creek gold mine.

rivers in the Interior. Douglas unilaterally extended his rule from Vancouver Island and the Charlottes to the mainland and announced regulations to govern the movement of men and supplies. This gave him some control over, and information about, the miners he expected from below the border. By the spring of 1858 the native people in the Interior had found about 800 ounces of gold and traded it to the Hudson's Bay Company. The nearest mint was in San Francisco and so a company ship, the *Otter*, took the gold there.

The news was out and the rush began. Soldiers left United States Army posts in Northwest Washing-

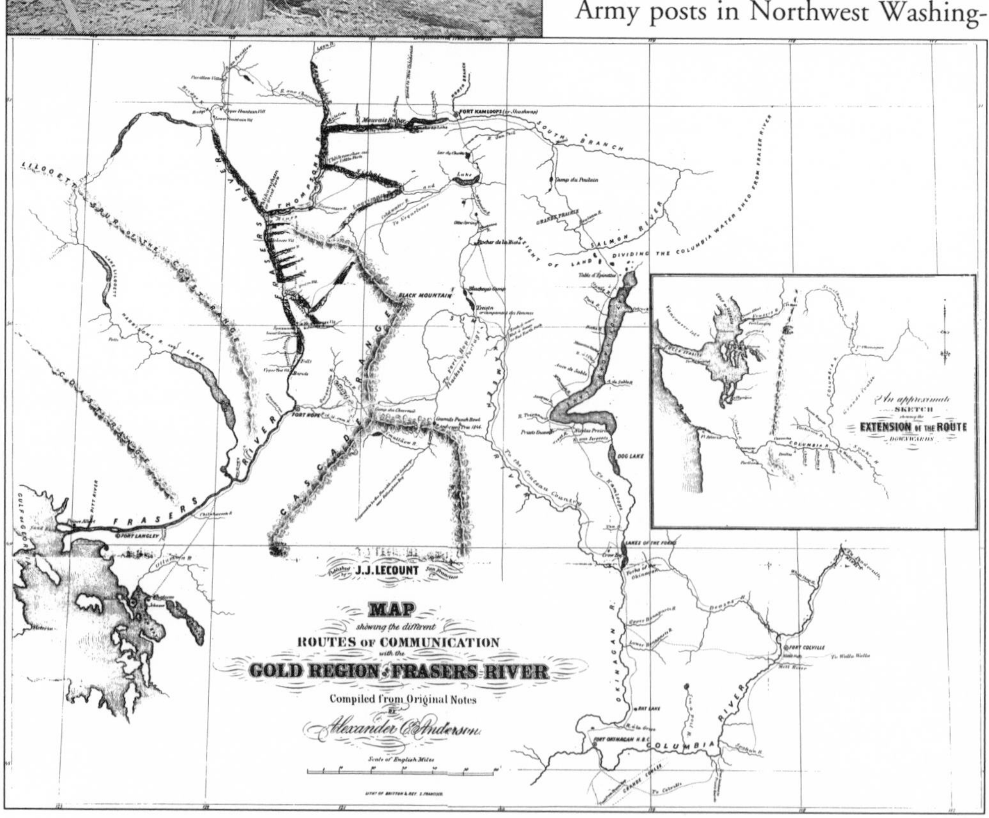

Error-filled map published in 1858 in San Francisco for would-be gold-miners.

ton; ship crews deserted; shopkeepers and banks lost staff. Some Americans came overland to the Fraser Valley around Lytton, Yale and Hope where the first substantial finds were made. But most came to Victoria from California by ship; the *Commodore's* arrival on April 25 was just the first. During April, May, June and July, about 16,000 people left California for Victoria and the Fraser. Among them was a large contingent of black people who were fleeing racial restrictions in California. Other prospectors came from Hawaii, South America, Eastern Canada, Europe and the United States. There are no exact figures, but one estimate is that about 30,000 people reached the Fraser in 1858. Most came first to Victoria, which was transformed from a small settlement around the fort into a tent and shack town devoted to housing and supplying the miners.

After a few days, they crossed Georgia Strait in any kind of boat or ship they could find to reach the new settlements and goldfields. Over the next few years, as the Fraser Canyon gold finds grew smaller, the men moved eastward to the Similkameen and the Thompson and then north up to the Cariboo and Barkerville. One 100-foot claim is said to have produced more than 100 ounces of gold in one day, worth about $1,600 (price today: about $36,000).

The arrival of massive numbers of Americans onto land claimed and controlled by Britain made Westminster listen to Douglas's warnings. On August 2, 1858, the bill turning New Caledonia into the colony of British Columbia got Royal As-

Matthew Baillie Begbie was a 39-year-old barrister in England when he left for B.C. He personified law and order in the new colony and rode on circuit, like British judges, and held trials when and where they were needed. Not a wisp of scandal soiled his reputation for fairness and integrity. In his first 13 years as a judge, he hanged 27 men; 22 were natives. In 1884, he did his best to thwart Ottawa's ban on native potlatch ceremonies and feasts by ruling against the Indian Act amendments in his courts. The legislation was re-written so that he was powerless. Begbie died in Victoria in 1894.

sent in London. The Colonial Office had recruited a mini-bureaucracy to manage the new colony and during the summer of 1858, Matthew Baillie Begbie, Chartres Brew and Colonel Richard Moody arrived in Victoria.

Begbie, 6 foot-4 inches, with a massive black beard, was appointed judge of the colony and soon started taking English-style justice to the settlements and gold fields. He worked with the Inspector of Police and Chief Gold Commissioner Chartres Brew, another man of power and integrity, who organized a system of constables, magistrates and courts that gave the goldfields and first settlements a simple but vigorous and sensible justice system.

Colonel Richard Moody came to the new colony in

Lieutenant Colonel Richard Moody, 45 years old, came to B.C. from a command in Malta. Earlier he had been Governor of the Falkland Islands. In B.C., he held three posts: Commander of the B.C. Detachment, Royal Engineers; Lieutenant Governor; and Chief Commissioner of Lands and Works. His men helped police the goldfields, and laid out New Westminster as the capital city. As well, they built roads and did surveying from their camp called Sapperton, named after the popular name for British army engineers—Sappers. In 1863, the Royal Engineers detachment was disbanded. Many of the men settled in B.C., but Moody, by now a wealthy land-owner, went back to England. He died in 1887.

command of 172 Royal Engineers whose task was to survey the land, lay out sites for cities and build trails or roads. But they were also soldiers. The dust raised by the flood of Americans coming to seek gold was not the only ominous cloud in the sky over the border. In 1859, the United States Army—soon to be engaged in a civil war that would cost a million lives—crushed the native people in Washington Territory to make room for new settlers. A body of trained soldiers, even a small one like the Engineers, was useful to have in the new colony at such a time.

The black community of Victoria was anxious to thank Governor Douglas for his welcome to them as they fled from racial prejudice in the United States. In 1860, when tension over control of the San Juan Islands was at its height, the community formed the Victoria Pioneer Rifle Company, popularly called the African Rifles. Members drilled and paraded in colourful uniforms sent over from England, but they never left Victoria.

The place of native people in the new British Columbia did not change as traumatically as did that of the native people south of the border. There was fighting between native people and Europeans in the fur-trading days but the incidents were limited and isolated. The easy-going relationship between the fur traders and the native people, based on mutual needs (the traders wanted furs and the native people could supply them) and the shared hardships of life in the forests and on river banks, changed as fur traders were replaced by gold miners and settlers. Now the native people were rivals for gold and land, not allies. The miners and settlers were not employees of firms with policies about relations with native people but entrepreneurs, out for all they could get and willing to kill for it. And the moderating influence of native women—wives, concubines and helpers to the fur traders—was lost. Now native women were stolen, abused and mistreated.

This was the time, too, of the Pig War—a dispute between British Columbia and a cocky American administration, first over a slaughtered pig, and then about the control of the San Juan Islands on the border between Vancouver Island and the mainland. Governor Douglas, happy to have both the Royal Navy's Pacific Squadron at Esquimalt and the Engineers at hand, and buoyed by a ferment of patriotism in the people of Victoria, wanted action. But the Navy advised caution, and the dispute was settled by the German Emperor 13 years later—in favour of the Americans.

Gold had galvanized the colony into life. Missionaries and teachers arrived to care for the spirit and mind. Settlers began to farm around Victoria and then on Saltspring

Island and in the Cowichan Valley. To feed the gold miners, settlers started farms on the banks of the Fraser River served by river steamers. In the Okanagan, along the old fur trail, cattle ranching and orchard growing began. Other ranches were built in the Thompson and Nicola valleys. The first sawmill had started work near Victoria in the late 1840s. In 1858, the first mill on the mainland was built at Yale to prepare lumber for the gold fields and settlements. And in the early 1860s the first mills started work on the north and south shores of Burrard Inlet. Most of the lumber exported went to Asia, Latin America, Australia and New Zealand. High tariffs and competitive pricing effectively closed the United States market. But at the end of the 1860s gold still made up 75% of the colony's exports by value. Lumber and furs each made up 10%, and coal, discovered in 1849 at Fort Rupert on the northern tip of Vancouver Island and then extensively mined at Nanaimo in the next few years, made up 5%.

Links with the outside world grew stronger. Victoria's harbour was the centre of a network of shipping routes that ran across to the Fraser and south to San Francisco with

Many settlers—and quite a few former gold miners—started farms on Vancouver Island, the Lower Mainland, and in the Okanagan. Land was cheap, often free, and the growing settlements wanted fresh food. Typical crops were potatoes, hay, oats, barley, wheat, turnips, and fruit. But soil quality varied—from the black loam of Delta, to the sandy soils of parts of the Fraser Valley, to the rocky, dry land of the Okanagan. Few farmers did well; most just scrimped a living, and many saw their dreams wither away.

An early view of Victoria Harbour, looking from the present business district towards the site of the Legislature. The inlet in the foreground was filled in at the turn of the century and the Empress Hotel was built here. Painting is Inner Harbour, Victoria*—by E.M. Richardson.*

connections there to the United States and the rest of the world. By 1864, the telegraph had reached the Pacific coast and communication with London took hours rather than weeks.

The flow of settlers now came overland. In the late summer of 1862 a group of 160 men, women and children left Fort Garry (now Winnipeg) in wagons on their way overland to the Cariboo goldfields. They ran out of food by the time they reached the Thompson and winter was coming so they had to make the last part of the journey on river rafts. They reached Kamloops in late October and a few hours later one of the party, Catherine Schubert, gave birth to a daughter called Rose, the first white child born on the mainland. Also in the party was an English Pre-Raphaelite artist, William Hind, who spent the next seven years painting gold miners and settlements and Victoria.

But settlement and industry grew too slowly and the shallow-rooted economic bloom generated by the gold rush began to wither. New political arrangements were necessary. Governor Douglas was getting old and new men were needed. Three stood out in the next few years:

The mother of the first white baby born on the mainland, Catherine Schubert came to B.C. with the Overlanders. She later told her family that while she was on the raft coming down the Thompson she wanted to get to a settlement before her labour started so that she would have another woman to help her. She succeeded—within a few hours of reaching Kamloops, she gave birth to a daughter, with a native woman there to help her.

European women were few and far between on the Mainland when Catherine Schubert gave birth. A good guess would suggest that there were 1,800 European women in what we now know as B.C., and most of them lived on Vancouver Island. The number of men was approximately 5,000.

Dr. John Helmcken, Amor De Cosmos and John Robson.

Helmcken, born in 1824, was trained in London as a doctor. A son-in-law of Douglas, he was pressed into political service soon after he arrived at Esquimalt in March 1850. He became Speaker of Vancouver Island's Legislative Assembly in 1856 and served until he was elected to the British Columbia Legislative Council after union with the mainland. In 1870 he was one of B.C.'s three delegates to settle the terms of Confederation.

Amor De Cosmos was born William Smith in Nova Scotia in 1825 and came to Victoria with gold miners from California in 1858. He stayed close to the fort, however, and started the *British Colonist.*

Another newspaper, the New Westminster *British Columbian,* was started in 1861 by the third man. John Robson was born in 1824 in Ontario and came to British Columbia in 1859. After the capital of B.C. was moved to Victoria from New Westminster, Robson followed in 1869 to be the editor of De Cosmos's *British Colonist.* He

Prospector Panning for Gold, Cariboo, *a painting by William Hind. He was a young British artist who came with the Overlanders in 1862 and stayed to paint before returning to Britain. The first artists who recorded life and scenery on the Pacific coast were members of Spanish and British expeditions. Eighty years later, other artists—both amateur and professional—came to paint and sketch, to be awed by the majesty of the mountains and fascinated by the seemingly strange life of the native people. Gradually, engravings and photographs took over the task of portraying and preserving B.C. for the world.*

fought for responsible and representative government and for Confederation, and served on both the Legislative Council and Legislature. Robson left newspapers and politics in 1875 to become paymaster for the surveyors laying out the CPR. In 1882 he was again a member of the Legislature, serving as Minister of Finance and Agriculture, and then as Premier from 1889. He died in 1892.

Amor De Cosmos worked in the California mines as a photographer. Some parts of his life are a mystery, but he told friends that he had changed his name to reflect his love of mankind. His enemies said that he had to change his name and that he left California in a hurry. Soon after his arrival, De Cosmos started the British Colonist *newspaper, as well as a long campaign against Governor Douglas. De Cosmos wanted responsible government and fought for democracy on the Island's Legislative Assembly and the B.C. Legislative Council. He was a powerful supporter of union with Canada and organised the Confederation League which met at Yale in September 1868. But his eccentricity and sarcasm had alienated many people and less controversial men were chosen to negotiate the terms of Confederation in Ottawa in the summer of 1870. De Cosmos was still popular with the voters, however, and he was later elected a federal MP and named Provincial Premier.*

Slowly the parts of the puzzle were put, or pushed, into place. Douglas retired in 1864 and the new governor from England, Frederick Seymour, pressed for the merger of the two debt-ridden colonies of Vancouver Island and British Columbia. It came on August 2, 1866, but did little to solve the economic crisis.

British Columbians had three choices:

- Stay a British colony and hope for more help but less control.
- Join the United States.
- Join the rest of Canada.

The first was unattractive, for the Colonial Office showed little sympathy for the desires and needs of an insignificant colony halfway around the world.

The second seemed attractive, for the U.S. Civil War was over and prosperity was moving swiftly across the plains to the Pacific. Petitions advocating joining the United States circulated in Victoria where most of the businesses had been started by Americans. The United States consul in Victoria sent Washington encouraging dispatches.

The third did not make much sense. After all, British Columbia was separated from Canada by thousands of miles of trackless waste.

Then, in March 1867, the U.S. bought Alaska from Russia for $7,200,000. Was B.C. trapped between two massive tracts of U.S. territory? Three months later the

Anthony Musgrave was the Governor of Newfoundland when the British Colonial Office appointed him to succeed Governor Seymour. He was a friend of Sir John A. Macdonald and known as a supporter of B.C. joining Canada. An affable, jolly man, Musgrave was instructed to make certain that B.C.'s Legislative Council voted in favour of Confederation; he quickly realized that money and a railway link were the keys. He told Ottawa and London that cash grants, pensions for administrators who would lose their jobs, and a railway would do the trick. Ottawa, pressed by London, accepted his advice.

provinces in the east joined in a Confederation and started to extend control over the land between Ontario and British Columbia. Would Canada be a better saviour now?

Amor De Cosmos formed the Confederation League in 1868, and John Robson joined him. In 1869, Governor Seymour, weakened by years of relentless drinking, died from dysentery. The new governor, Anthony Musgrave, arrived from Newfoundland with Colonial office orders to speed up the union with Canada. In the bars and homes of Victoria, New Westminster and the other tiny settlements, the arguments were fierce and long. The Legislative Council in Victoria, spurred on by Musgrave and after seemingly endless debate, agreed to terms proposed by the governor.

Musgrave picked three delegates to go to Ottawa to propose the terms of joining Confederation. On May 14, 1870, Dr. John Helmcken, Lands Commissioner John Trutch, his wife, Amelia and Dr. Robert Carrall from the Cariboo, sailed from Victoria to San Francisco on their way to Ottawa.

On A Transcontinental Train

May 22, 1870

It's a bright, sunny afternoon and the Central Pacific wood-burning locomotive is steaming hard to keep time as it crosses Nevada on the way to Promontory, Utah. Behind the locomotive, the sleeping cars—part of the train that left Sacramento in California the day before—are almost full. Most of the passengers are still so engrossed by the scenery of the Sierra Nevada range that they are quietly looking outwards, ignoring their fellow passengers.

But one group, a woman and three men, only occasionally glance out the window; these four are busy arguing. Amelia Trutch, her husband Joseph, Dr. John Helmcken and Dr. Robert Carrall, are from Victoria, British Columbia, about 900 miles to the north. The three men are delegates of the colony on their way to Ottawa—the capital of the new Dominion of Canada—to negotiate the terms of British Columbia's union with Canada. They left Victoria a week ago in a wooden paddle steamer, the *Active*, and spent a few days shopping and enjoying life

Central Pacific train in the Nevada Sierra.

in San Francisco. Yesterday they boarded a ferry which took them over the bay to Oakland and to the start of their railway journey across half the continent.

Dr. Helmcken is talking. He practices as a doctor but Helmcken has spent much of the time since he arrived in Victoria from England as an administrator and politician. He is a widower; his wife, Cecilia, one of Governor Douglas's daughters, died five years ago, leaving him with three young children.

No, he's not worried about the children, he tells Mrs. Trutch. They are well taken care of. Helmcken says he's more worried about the antics of Mr. Henry Seelye, one of the editors of Victoria's *Daily Colonist* who came with the party from Victoria but who caught a train to the east a day earlier. Seelye would be in Ottawa before the delegates, Helmcken points out. God only knows what he'll say to the government in Ottawa. Seelye appointed himself a delegate, Helmcken protests. He had been put up to it by John Robson, Seelye's partner at the *Daily Colonist* and a fervent advocate of joining the Canadian confederation. Helmcken leans forward in his seat and looks hard at Dr. Carrall and Mr. Trutch. It was obviously a part of their underhanded campaign.

When B.C. joined Canada on July 20, 1871, there had to be elections for the six M.P.'s seats and for the 25 seats in the new legislature. Most Victorians assumed John Helmcken would run for one of the seats. Joseph Trutch, the first Lieutenant-Governor, asked Helmcken if he would form the provincial government. But Helmcken decided he would spend his time with his young family and resume his practice. He was the founder of the B.C. Medical Association and was named its first president in 1885. He started to write his memoirs, and was a familiar figure with his pony and trap as he travelled about to see his patients. Helmcken died in Victoria in 1920. He was 96.

But now the tiny Central Pacific train has stopped to let the passengers get a meal. The carriages are the latest in luxury—the Central Pacific and Union Pacific, which have operated the transcontinental railroad out of Omaha, Nebraska, for a year, are determined to surround the first-class passengers on the fashionable transcontinental run with mirrors, satins, rosewood and maple. Quite a change for passengers from the dusty, spartan stages. There are no dining cars, however, so the passengers, including the British Columbians, get out and take their pick of antelope steaks, beef steaks, chicken, poached eggs, potatoes, corn and hot cakes—washed down with coffee.

As soon as the locomotive's tender is filled with water and four-foot logs, the train is off. Carrall and Trutch pick up the argument with Helmcken. You know as well as we do what Robson and Seelye are doing, says Carrall. They want to make certain that the Canadians require the establishment of a some form of responsible, representative goverment as a condition of our joining Confederation. If the Canadians don't make this a condition of agreeing to British Columbia's terms, Robson and Seelye will use the *Colonist's* columns to make certain they get their way. That's the message Seelye will be taking, and—of course—he'll be telegraphing back reports of what we're doing in Ottawa.

Carrall is no lover of American political institutions such as responsible and representative government. He was born in Woodstock, Ontario and was a surgeon in the Union Army during the American Civil War. Then he settled in Barkerville in the Cariboo, practiced medicine there and soon became involved in politics, serving as the elected member for Cariboo in the quasi-elective Legislative Council. He is a proud Canadian who wants British Columbia to be part of a Canada stretching from coast to coast.

Trutch, the other advocate of confederation, is a colonial official—B.C.'s Commissioner of Lands and Works. He is an Englishman who has worked as a civil engineer in Illinois and Oregon. He met Colonel R. C. Moody, of the Royal Engineers, in England, followed him to British Columbia and built roads and the Alexandra suspension bridge over the Fraser. Wealthy, he is one of many who have tried to re-create

THE BRITISH COLONIST

Wednesday Morning, July 20, 1870

PORT OF VICTORIA, BRITISH COLUMBIA

The Terms of Union

Under date Ottawa June 27th the Special Correspondent of the Toronto *Globe* furnishes that paper with the following conditions, which it is claimed were 'received on authority':—

Canada is to assume the debts and liabilities of British Columbia up to the date of Union. The population limit for the purpose of financial arrangements shall be fixed at 100,000.

The British Columbia debt shall be assumed to be $3,000,000. The colony to receive interest at the rate of 5 per cent, per annum, payable half-yearly in advance, on the difference between the assumed debt and the actual debt. The actual debt is $1,000,000.

The annual grant for the support of British Columbia Local Government and Legislature to be $35,000. A guarantee of interest at 6 per cent, on an outlay not exceeding $500,000 for the construction of a graving dock in the harbor of Esquimalt was asked, and stands over for consideration and negotiations.

The expense of all the Federal services as provided by the B N A Act to be assumed by the Dominion Government.

Pensions to be granted to all of Her Majesty's servants now in the service of the Crown colony who may lose their salaries and emoluments in consequence of the colony entering the Union; such pensions being subject to the approval of Her Majesty's Government. Regular steam communication between Victoria and San Francisco to be maintained fortnightly by two British steamers.

The Dominion Government to guarantee the construction as early as practicable of a railroad across the continent—with the western terminus at a port in British Columbia on the Pacific Coast, and connecting in the east with the railroad system of Canada, in Western Canada. This great railroad is estimated to cost, in round figures, $100,000,000. Offers to build it are made to the government on the basis of a grant of alternate sections of land on each side of the road—one mile long and twelve deep, and a guarantee at 6 per cent interest on debentures redeemable in twenty years. British Columbia to be represented in the House of Commons by six representatives, instead of eight, as demanded, and, it is stated, by three senators instead of four.

The government guarantees that the whole of the public officials appointed for the carrying out of the new government shall be in every way acceptable to the people. The expressed wishes of the people of British Columbia for responsible representative government (to obtain which Mr. Seelye came with the delegates) are conceded. The tariff of the Dominion will be extended over the colony and the present British Columbian tariff, which it was sought to retain, will be discountinued.

The remaining terms are unimportant. They refer to the extension of the postal service, the erection of an Hospital, a Lunatic Asylum, and a Penitentiary, Protection of the Fisheries, aid to Immigration, the election of Senators, the formal admission of the colony in to the Union, the defense of the colony and aid to the volunteer force—in all of which requirements the delegates declare themselves to be perfectly well satisfied.

The correspondent of the *Globe*, while admitting that 'the delegates are not authorized to make public the result of their mission,' claims to have received the above 'on authority.' Without waiting to reconcile the apparent paradox we may say that, with, perhaps, one or two exceptions, the *Globe's* terms will be found substantially correct.

The Colonist *tells its readers about terms of union.*

Victorian England around Victoria. Like Carrall, Trutch is no lover of American institutions, fears annexation by the U.S. and so wants B.C. to join Confederation.

Helmcken, Trutch says, it's you I worry about—not Seelye. After all, you've flirted with annexation and you've never concealed your disdain for Canadians. What's your phrase? Yes—North American Chinamen, you call them. I find it hard to make up my mind where you stand on all the terms we've been told to discuss—the money we need to pay our debts, the future of the colonial officials like myself, those ridiculously low Canadian tariffs and, of course, the link between British Columbia and Canada.

The train is running along the Humboldt River. After a glance at the forlorn landscape, Helmcken tells the two men that his views of the terms of union are simple. If Ottawa agrees to grant enough money—based on his plan to double the colony's population from 30,000 to 60,000 for per capita grants—and to look after the officials and the farmers in a generous fashion, then he would look favourably on union.

But what about the railway and wagon road? Trutch asks. I believe you've supported the idea of a railway for a perverse reason. I think that you believe the idea of a railway is so ridiculous that Sir John A. will reject it and the whole parcel of terms

THE INLAND SENTINEL

YALE, THURSDAY, MARCH 9, 1882

The C.P.R. Railway

It is confidently stated that the C.P.R. engineers have found a practicable route through the Rocky and Selkirk Mountain ranges, nearly 200 miles south of the Yellowhead Pass. By the bargain the Company are bound to carry the railway through the Yellowhead. It will therefore be necessary for them to get there from Parliament to use the more southerly pass. Should this be as good as reported they will doubtless apply for new legislation. Their line is about as far from Kamloops—where it must go—as from the Yellowhead Pass. Leave to use the newly discovered route would save the Company the necessity of constructing something like 200 miles of railway north-westerly from Calgary to Yellowhead at a cost of perhaps $20, 000 a mile, as this piece of line would a traverse a rolling country much cut up by rivers.

Were the Company to accept a reduction of their subsidy equal to the amount they will save by obtaining leave to use the southern pass, something could be said in favor of granting this concession. Otherwise it will be advisable to hold them to their bargain and the Yellowhead route. It is not desirable that the mountain section should be near the American frontier, where it could be easily seized by an American force. The consideration is not without weight where the country has a choice between a road that can be not be defended at the same price. In the course of a few years there will be line across the prairies far north of the Canada Pacific, and if the Yellowhead Pass were used by the latter the country would have a good military route to British Columbia via the northerly prairie road. To let the C.P.R. use the southerly pass without paying for the privilege will be to gain nothing, and to deprive Canada of a transcontinental line out of American reach.

Again the C.P.R. section between Calgary and Yellowhead would afford railway facilities to t fertile district and conduce much to its early settlement. To let the Company use the southerly pass will be to throw the burden of constructing a railway two hundred miles long through that fertile district on other capitalists, and as the Government would, doubtless, aid them with the usual land subsidy, something like 800,000 acres of land would be lost to the public. Saving about $8,000,000 in construction by changing the Eastern Section location to Ontario's disadvantage, the Syndicate can very well afford to stick their bargain and the Yellowhead Pass. Parliament should, therefore, not make a new concession without getting a full equivalent for it."
THOMPSON RIVER

Arguments about the CPR's route went on until work began in 1881. Finally, it took the southern route across the Prairies and through Kicking Horse Pass rather than going to the north and crossing the mountains through Yellowhead Pass.

will fall apart.

Helmcken smiles. He has been reading all about the railway they are riding on, he tells Trutch and Carrall. How the government gave the contractors about $30,000 a mile and massive land grants and government bonds and then swindled the Indians out of millions of acres of land. How they got thousands of Chinese men to do the dirty work while Irishmen and veterans of both the Union and Confederate armies laid the track and spiked the rails. And all about the way they solved the problems of building bridges and tracks in snow, ice and the desert. Just look at this car we're riding in and then look outside and see how fast we're moving. If this guidebook he bought in San Francisco is right, says Helmcken, warming to his subject, we're travelling at more than 20 miles an hour. As far as he is concerned, if Canada will build a railway as good as this one, that alone would be reason to join Canada—provided there's none of the massive swindling of ordinary people and Indians that has happened here.

Helmcken has become so excited that the other passengers are all listening and looking at him. But then the locomotive's whistle shrieks and cuts short his little speech. There will be other arguments but for now the four British Columbians are thinking of what 's ahead. Soon they will be in Promontory, Utah, where the last spike of the transcontinental railroad had been driven a year earlier. There they will be joining a Union Pacific train that will take them through the Wyoming Rockies and along the old Oregon trail to Omaha. The Rock Island line will then whisk them to Chicago and the Michigan Central to Detroit. And then a Canadian railroad, the Great Western, will take them into Canada.

LIVING ON THE EDGE 1871 to 1900

For Wealthy Women: Babies and Fine Clothes

For Poor Women: Babies and Hard Work

Disease and Despair Attack Native People

Newspapers Open Up Communication

AROUND THE WORLD
England — 1878 Methodist preacher William Booth founds Salvation Army
Germany — 1885 Daimler builds first gasoline-powered motorcycle
South Africa — 1899 360,000 British troops face 100,000 Boers

POPULATION — 1881		
Native People	25,661	(52%)
British	14,660	(29%)
Other Europeans	2,490	(5%)
Asians	4,350	(9%)
Other	2,298	(5%)
Total	49,459	

*ethnic origin

John Helmcken came back to Victoria on July 18, 1870 and told Governor Musgrave about the delegates' success in Ottawa. The other delegates, Carrall and Trutch, had followed what was to be a familiar pattern for British Columbia politicians: they added on some personal visiting at the end of their official trip east. Mr. and Mrs. Trutch went to England and Carrall went back to his home in Ontario. Helmcken found that he could tell Musgrave little new. After all, Seelye had been sending back despatches from Ottawa to the *British Colonist* as well as lobbying for a more democratic government for British Columbia. And official despatches had kept Musgrave informed about the talks.

British Columbia was promised what it had asked for. London was eager to be rid of a colony 6,000 miles away and made certain that the new dominion made the new province welcome. True, grants were to be based on a fictitious population of 60,000, but

Society in B.C. in the nineteenth century was sharply focused on the family. Individuals—particularly women—bereft of family support were virtual outsiders. Only in family activities could women achieve any power or status. Large families for the middle class meant care in their old age; for the poor they meant more income as children were sent out to work.

Vancouver Prices — 1887	
Flour	*$6.00/barrel*
Rice	*$2.00/sack*
Bacon	*$0.15/pound*
Coffee	*$0.30/pound*
Steak	*$0.15/pound*
Mutton	*$0.15/pound*
Cod	*$0.05/pound*
Salmon	*$0.65/each*

that loss was matched by Ottawa's generosity in promising construction of a railway to the coast starting in ten years or earlier.

British Columbia had asked for a wagon road and then a railway. Now the railway was to be started at both ends, like the American transcontinental, so that the new province would get benefits at the beginning. And Seelye's work had made John Robson, Amor De Cosmos and the other advocates of political freedom happy. Ottawa had made it clear that British Columbia was to start its life as a province of Canada with responsible government and a fully-elected legislature.

Many Victorians were not so easily pleased. You were tricked, Helmcken was told by people he met in the street. The railway would never be built. Canadians were too stingy. And why won't Victoria be the terminus? But when the Legislative Council met on January 5, 1871, they approved the terms of union unanimously. Strangely, none of the delegates got any recognition or thanks from their fellow British Columbians. Carrall was made a senator by Ottawa, however, and Trutch was feted in the capital and made the province's first lieutenant-governor.

Helmcken went back to work as a doctor.

The new province's society was typically colonial—the native people were in a majority, the Europeans a minority, and women an even smaller group. About 30% of the Europeans who lived on the tip of Vancouver Island and in New Westminster were female. Women made up about 10% of the settlers living in the Interior. Their style of living (the women and their husbands, for there were virtually no unmarried females over 25) was determined by wealth and social status. In the cities of Victoria and, to a lesser extent, New Westminster, the middle class tried to recreate the life they had left behind, or that their parents had told them about. Respectability and propriety were paramount. Families were relatively large because any kind of contraception was secret and regarded as immoral. As in the industrial society they had left behind, middle class women performed virtually no work outside the home. Bearing and nurturing children, running the home, supporting their husbands, and appearing decorative to bolster their husbands' social position—these were their duties.

Fashionable clothes for the middle-class woman came from London and San Francisco and the new fabrics, colours and designs made possible by advances in spinning, weaving and dyeing were available in Victoria a few months after appearing in Paris and London. The British Colonist *ran advertisements for all kinds of clothing when shipments arrived in port. For women with less money, such as the wives of coal miners at Nanaimo, a local dressmaker made clothes in poorer fabrics and just a few years behind the fashion in style and colour.*

Women whose husbands had less money led less restricted—but also harder—lives. Many of them played active roles in farming and ranching and for them childbearing was just an added task. Although childbed was becoming less dangerous, the chance of losing a baby in the first years was still high. Children's diseases, the low immunity of children to all kinds of disease, and the sorry state of medical science meant that parents lived in fear until the children reached 15 years or so. Amelia Douglas,

Painter Emily Carr—bottom right, with her sisters—on Dr. Helmcken, in the early 1880s:

"Dr. Helmcken attended to all our ailments—Father's gout, our stomach-aches; he even told us what to do once when the cat had fits.... You began to get better the moment you heard (him) coming up the stairs. He did have the most horrible medicines—castor oil, Gregory's powder, blue pills, black draughts, sulphur and treacle.... Once I knelt on a needle which broke into my knee.... The Doctor cut slits in my knee and wiggled his fingers round inside it for three hours hunting for the pieces of needle. The Doctor said, 'Yell, lassie, yell! It will let the pain out.'.... I remember the Doctor's glad voice as he said, 'Thank God, I have got all of it now, or the lassie would have been lame for life....' Then he washed his hands under the kitchen tap and gave me a peppermint." (From The Book of Small. *Toronto, 1942.)*

the governor's wife, gave birth to 13 children, but only five survived her.

Medicine had progressed slowly and although surgery, antiseptics and simple drugs were available by this time, diagnosis was difficult, medical information scanty and training very poor. Dr. Helmcken told how he was reluctant to use carbolic acid as an antiseptic for Governor Musgrave when he broke his ankle and blamed the governor's permanent lameness on another doctor who used it profusely. Outside the cities, medical help was virtually non-existent and only family remedies were there to help.

By the mid-seventies the largest city, Victoria, saved from economic ruin when the capital was moved from New Westminster in 1868, had shed all the traces of the late fifties and its role as the base for thousands of miners and prospectors. Many of the Americans who had come in the gold-rush days had gone back to the United States to enjoy the prosperity that followed the end of the Civil War and the contruction of the railroads in the West. There were still about 5,000 people living in the city. Now the shacks had gone and Victoria's buildings were built of stone and brick; the streets were paved, and lit by gas.

Government Street, Victoria, 1866.

There were still too many saloons for staid Victorians, and quite a few provided rooms for prostitutes up the stairs. There were around 80 billiard tables—one for every 70 people! Contemporary quote: "The average Victorian's sense of bliss apparently consists of the largest possible number of drinks in the shortest possible time, varied with cigars and billiards ad lib."

Social life for the city's elite was staid and predictable. The presence of the Royal Navy's Pacific Squadron provided genteel competition for the company of young women at the balls and parties that filled the social season. The Theatre Royal provided a home for touring companies and local amateurs and a Philharmonic Society offered concerts and recitals for music-lovers. Tennis courts were necessities for the wealthy, encouraged by Chief Justice Baillie Begbie, who gave the best tennis parties.

A school system with central control had been planned under Governor Douglas but a shortage of money hampered progress. After Confederation, John Jessop was appointed school superintendent and in 1872 he introduced legislation for a school system with free universal education that has been the measure ever since. A Central High School was opened in 1877. Jessop even set his sights on a university. Some university degrees were awarded through arrangements with McGill in Montreal in the late nineteenth century but the University of B.C. did not open until 1915.

First-year university courses had been offered in Vancouver since 1899. Work on the University of B.C.'s campus on Point Grey was stopped during the first World War, however, and buildings were left unfinished. In 1922, students and sympathizers protested in the Great Trek; they climbed the skeleton of the Science Building. The building was finished one year later.

Anglican, Roman Catholic and Methodist ministers followed the first settlers to Vancouver Island. They had two objectives: to provide schools and pastoral services to the Hudson's Bay officers, men and the settlers; and to

The church is the social centre of the European community. Here, it's 1908 and the newly-wedded couple are coming out of Christ Church, Vancouver. For the crowd outside, many who have come on bicycle, now's the chance to congratulate, and enjoy the occasion.

convert the native people to Christianity. First in the Victoria area was Father Modeste Demers, named Bishop of Vancouver Island in 1847. An Anglican, Reverend Robert Staines arrived two years later with his wife to run a boarding school and give Anglican services. In 1858 four sisters of St. Anne came from Quebec to set up Catholic schools in Victoria and New Westminster. By the 1860s, a Methodist minister was paddling a canoe up the Fraser River to preach to the gold miners. A synagogue was soon built in Victoria. As settlers opened up the Lower Mainland and the Interior, the churches moved with them.

The churches preached a social gospel, too. In 1862 and 1863 the Anglicans, realising that a society so poorly supplied with women lacked stability, brought over two bride ships to Victoria. Records are scanty but it's difficult to call the experiment successful. Some women married settlers, but others joined the local prostitutes. In 1862 William Duncan—an Anglican appalled by the effects of European society on the native people living north of what is now Prince Rupert—persuaded them to move to a Utopia-like community, called Metlakatla. The churches were ardent supporters of the potlatch ban in 1884 as part of their campaign to persuade native people to adopt European value or habits. And in the early years of the next century, churches were active fighters for temperance, women's suffrage, and social and workplace reform. This

Many diseases, such as measles, TB, smallpox, influenza, venereal diseases and alcoholism, were introduced to B.C. by Europeans. Most Europeans were immune to smallpox—the most deadly of the illnesses—by exposure or vaccination by the early nineteenth century. The native people were unprotected. A smallpox epidemic in Northern B.C. in 1780 nearly decimated the Tlingit and Haida communities, killing an estimated 60,000 native people. In Fort Simpson in 1836, about one-third of the Tsimshian population was destroyed. In 1860, in Victoria and along the coastal communities, another 20,000 native people died.

role was revived in the Depression and continues today.

As more settlers arrived, pressures on the traditional life of the native people increased. Many Europeans were convinced that they had a mission to bring their kind of civilisation to the aboriginals. What they saw of the native people who lived around the cities and settlements confirmed their prejudices: drunkenness, prostitution and disease had made some native people pathetic creatures whose plight wrung the hearts of missionaries and well-

Two views of spiritual life: Top, native people at a potlatch ceremony; bottom, native people dressed in European styles in front of a Christian church in Squamish, 189_.

Once settlers and miners arrived, native culture was under attack. Soon traditional costume vanished and European clothes became the norm. Chiefs who cooperated were given military-style uniforms. The nudity or semi-nudity of some native groups was disturbing to the over-clothed settlers and missionaries; they soon had women in long skirts and sweaters and men in jackets and trousers. Traditional dress—with its symbolic value—was reserved for private ceremonies.

The worst blow came in 1884 when the Indian Act was amended to ban the gift-giving and feasting of the potlatch. To the Europeans, these ceremonies were occasions for drunkenness, debauchery and paganism. For the natives, they were an integral part of the spiritual life that bonded them to the land, the creatures of the sea and forests, and to each other. Some groups held potlatch ceremonies in secret. When the ban was lifted in 1951, it took years to revive the ceremony.

A group of Chinese workers on the CPR. They were paid much less than the Europeans, did the most dangerous and menial tasks, and lived in the worst camps. But the CPR could not have been built without them.

intentioned matrons.

These were the outward and visible signs of the inward and spiritual corruption that had started at the beginning of the century. Unfortunately, the evangelical spirit, if not beliefs, of many of the settlers and new town dwellers encouraged the work of missionaries who tried to convert the native people to Christianity and a foreign—and for them, destructive—way of living.

Under Governor Douglas, the old fur trader, the native people had received sympathetic treatment. He tried to protect native villages, fishing places, hunting sites and fields against settlers because he believed that native people, if given the chance, could prosper at the side of the Europeans. But Douglas retired in 1864 and Joseph Trutch took over Indian Affairs as part of his job as commissioner of works. The protective shield around native settlements was broken and the whittling away of native lands and customs gathered speed.

The terms of union made Indian Affairs a federal responsibility and native leaders expected improvement for relationships with the native people were more sympathetically handled in the other provinces than they were in B.C. Native people made up about 70% of the population at this time but they were not involved in any political decisions. Despite, or perhaps because of, the appointment of federal Indian Affairs officers, the tensions between native people and settlers grew, chiefly over land and native women. The building of the Canadian Pacific railway in the province in the early 1880s made the situation worse.

On the shores of Vancouver Island, Burrard Inlet, and the rivers and lakes in the Interior, small mills like this one converted the logs cut nearby into construction lumber and planks. This is the North Pacific Lumber Company's mill in Barnet.

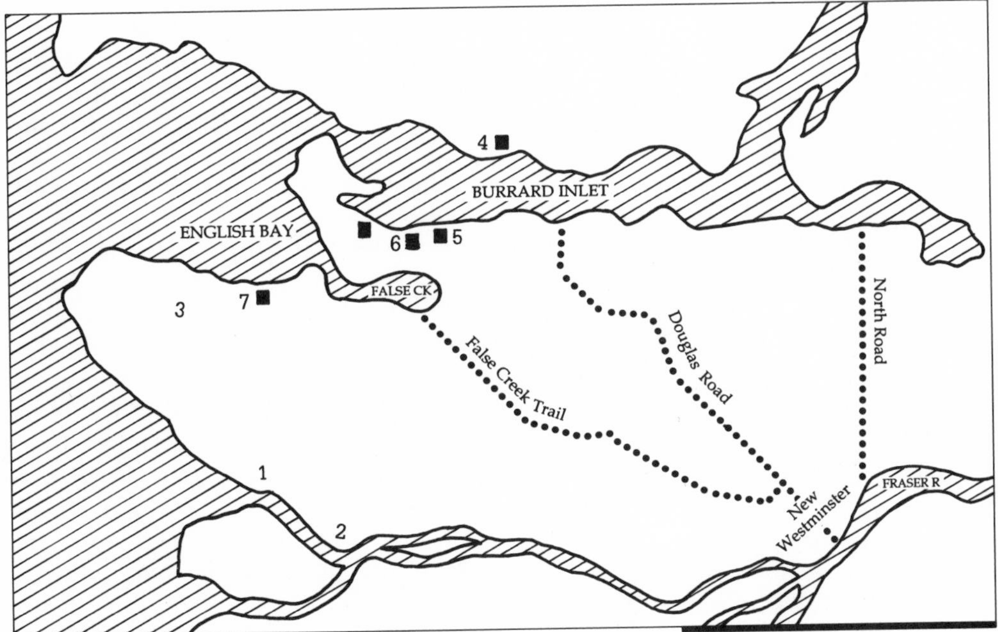

Native people received no compensation for the vast tracts of land given to the CPR and the construction camps became sinks of degradation for many native men and women.

Native people joined the Europeans in distrusting the Chinese, however. During the first ten years of Confederation, the number of Chinese people in the province doubled, and by 1881 there were around 4,000 Chinese people in the province. Chinese immigrants had first come to Victoria as part of the flood into the colony from the United States in 1858. Some followed the miners up the Fraser; others stayed to work as servants and laundrymen in Victoria where they were joined by hundreds sailing directly from Hong Kong. Their dress, reluctance to join in European society, and preference for opium rather than alcohol made them the victims of abuse and prejudice. Following the example of the builders of the U.S. transcontinental railroad, Contractor Andrew Onderdonk—short of labourers for the British Columbia section of the Canadian Pacific Railway—brought in 2,000 mainland Chinese in May 1881. By the time the line was finished in

First settlements on Burrard Inlet:
1. Musqueam village.
2. Great Fraser Midden.
First European settlements, 1860s:
3. John Morton's shack near present Marine Building.
4. Pioneer Mills, later Moody's.
5. Stamp's Mill on South shore under construction.
6. Gassy Jack opens saloon close to Stamp's Mill.
7. Jerry Rogers' Logging Camp at Jerry's Cove, now Jericho.

Buildings in Vancouver:

February 1886:	*100*
May 1886:	*800*

November 1885, more than two-thirds of the 13,000 men working on the railway were Chinese. When work on the railway stopped, most drifted back to the coast where they were a constant irritant to the burghers of Victoria and Vancouver.

Settlement depended on the economy and until work started on the railway, few new immigrants came to the province. But some small groups of men and their families started to live around the first sawmills, fish plants and mines. There were virtually no roads, no amenities or comforts. For men, women and children, life consisted of a daily struggle to keep dry, warm and get some simple food inside them. Food had to come from the sea, the river, their own gardens and small fields, and the forests. Hunting deer, rabbits and game brought a change to a monotonous diet. Many clothes, tools, utensils and items of furniture were hand-made, for there were few stores and usually no way to get to them. Social life, too, had to be handmade and centred around the church or school or one of the larger homes.

By the early 1880s there were about 200 people engaged in mixed farming in Langley, Delta and Richmond. About the same number tried to grow grain and raise cattle

The first passenger train from Montreal to the Pacific, headed by wood-burning locomotive No. 371, reached Port Moody at noon on July 4, 1886. About 1,500 people from the Island, New Westminster and Burrard Inlet came to picnic, listen to concerts and to greet the train and its passengers.

The settlement of Granville was incorpororated as the City of Vancouver on April 6, 1886. It was destroyed by fire two months later, on June 13. The blaze started in a clearing and quickly leapt from treetop to treetop until it surrounded the built-up area. Encouraged by a stiff breeze, the fire turned wooden buildings into instant bonfires. Most people escaped out of town or by wading out into the water. No-one knows how many died, but one estimate is 20 people. Rebuilding started the next morning.

in the Okanagan and Southern Interior. Lumbering, often a one-man or one-family operation, was confined to the coast where the giant logs, some up to nine feet thick, could be rolled into the water to be taken to the nearest mill. Most of the fish were caught by natives, but canneries opened in the 1870s and attracted European communities to places where the fish could be landed, cut, cleaned, boiled and canned as quickly as possible—the Fraser, Skeena and Nass estuaries. As the goldfields dwindled and communities such as Barkerville slowly became backwaters, other mining communties grew up in the Kootenays close to the U.S. border and smelters.

Slowly, too, small communities grew around Burrard Inlet, long recognised as a strategic centre for both military and economic purposes, and yet strangely deserted. The first settlement in what is now the Vancouver area came in September, 1862, when the McCleery family started farming on the north shore of the Fraser. In the same month, three disappointed miners decided to settle down in the area now known as the West End. By the late seventies, there were hotels, shacks, and mills on the shores of the inlet and two communities called Hastings and Granville. Only 700 or so people lived there.

That was soon to change. In May 1880 work began at Yale—about 120 miles to the east—on the British Columbia section of the railway that would turn Burrard Inlet and its tiny communities into a large city. Just over five years later, on November 7, 1885, the east and west tracks were joined at Craigellachie, in the mountains. And soon afterwards, the first train from the east arrived in Port Moody, a small village tucked away at the head of the inlet.

Port Moody was not the harbour the CPR wanted, however, for it was too shallow for ocean-going ships.

After the bustle of building the CPR, Yale sleeps in the mid-day sun in this 1890 photo. Like so many of the communities on the railway's route Yale was, for a few years, host to a motley crew of engineers, sailors, surveyors, tracklayers, labourers, and all those working in what is now called the service industry.

Granville was more like it and, after a gift of about 6,000 acres from the provincial government and some more from far-sighted local entrepreneurs, the CPR built tracks along the southern shore of Burrard Inlet. The boom that resulted rivalled the gold rush. Granville became the city of Vancouver on April 6, 1886, burned to the ground two months later and was rebuilt almost as fast. The city's rocket-like growth was fuelled by the arrival of the first passenger train from Montreal on May 23, 1887, and the docking of the first passenger ship from Asia, the *Abyssinia*, three weeks later.

In short order, real-estate men and engineers had the business and residential sections laid out, roads and sewers built and street lights turned on. Banks, hotels, business blocks and shops sprung up. Boarding houses and shacks filled up with the clerks and workers who would help the businessmen turn native forest into profitable asphalt jungle. Schools and an opera house followed. After all, nearly everyone in the city came from somewhere else and so all the trappings of the cities they had left behind had to be built to make Vancouver like home.

But visitors complained that the city lacked character; the only reasons for its existence were money and the CPR. Then street cars started running on routes carefully planned to favour CPR holdings. What was good for the CPR was good for Vancouver, it seemed. It had taken Victoria more than 40 years to go from settlement to city. Vancouver did it in less than one tenth of the time.

A Cabin In The Southern Interior

July 20, 1881

It's been ten years since British Columbia changed from a British colony to a Canadian province, but for the people who live in this log house in southeastern B.C., life has changed little.

The door is open and a woman is going in with a bucket of milk from a cow which is kept in the little lean-to at the back of the house. The floor is dirt; the walls are logs, rough-hewn to fit at the corners, with mud

Cabins like this give their families little more than shelter, warmth, and privacy…and a home.

and straw stuffed in the chinks and corners to keep out the rain and wind. Poles laid across the tops of the walls support a layer of one-foot-thick sod. It will keep in the heat and keep out a shower but heavy rains soon force a way through.

Inside, underneath the only window, is a table with two chairs and a bench, all hand-made from lumber cut and sawn from the trees nearby. The family—the woman's husband and their two daughters—are away in the small village selling eggs and butter. They hope to build a better house soon. Most of the logs to build it are already cut; they will try to dig a sawpit so that the logs can be cut into planks and rafters.

Behind the door is a large bunk made of a frame and a mattress filled with straw. The woman and her husband sleep here. Another, smaller bunk is in the opposite corner, close to the stove. The daughters, nine and eleven, sleep there. They pull the pillows over their heads and cuddle each other tighter when they hear strange noises outside in the night.

All the furniture has been made by the husband except for the wife's three prized possessions: the black iron wood stove her parents gave her; the china dresser set of water jug, soapdish and bowl on a small table between the beds; some tin canisters on a shelf over the stove. The stove burns wood in a grate flanked by an oven on one side and a hot water reservoir with a brass tap on the other. The canisters hold the only foods the family cannot gain from their land—flour, tea, coffee and salt.

The woman pours the milk into bowls on the table and covers them with cloths. When the cream has risen, she will skim it off and make butter by churning it by hand in a wooden bowl, taking care to tip out the water and add salt at the right times. Some skim milk she keeps for her family; the rest she gives to a neighbour for her pigs, getting some bacon in exchange.

The woman is thirty years old but already her face is drawn, her eyes wrinkled and her body lean. She is wearing the same kinds of clothes her mother wore: a cotton blouse and a long woollen brown skirt. The simple blouse is gathered at the neck and fastened with a cheap metal brooch. Her skirt is tied around her waist and underneath she wears a bodice, a petticoat and black stockings tied above her knees. On her feet—black leather boots. All the family's clothes are simple, for she has to wash them with home-made soap and rinse them in the nearby creek. Her husband wears woollen trousers and a coarse woollen shirt with woollen combinations underneath. On his feet, gumboots. The girls wear cotton dresses, dressed up to go out with coloured sashes, simple petticoats, white stockings and black boots.

Before she starts to prepare a meal for her family, she lets her chickens out of their run so that they can forage around the house. She trims the wick and fills the bowl of the family's only source of light—a kerosene lamp they bought last month. Until then, they used candles handmade from fat. Soon the children will be going to the new school in the village and will need a light for their lessons. Their mother can read and write a little and looks forward to getting a letter at the post office which has just opened in the village. Their father thinks learning a waste of time—especially for girls—but the woman will have her way.

She sits down a moment, wonders what to cook and smiles when she remembers her childhood and the way her mother often

Wherever a few homes were gathered together, a school was built. This is Eburne in 1908.

wondered how she could find anything to cook at all.

Well, she can go out to the lean-to and take some fish from the salting barrel, rinse them in the creek and then fry them to eat with the bread she baked yesterday. No, fish are best fresh. Better to wait until her husband catches fish in the creek. Keep the salted fish for hard times.

If the family comes back early, her husband can shoot some pheasants—but no, they should hang a little. Kill and eat that old broody hen that pecks your hand? No. Better to dip her in the creek to shake her out of her broodiness.

Only one thing left. She'll try to roast the haunch of venison from the deer her husband shot last week. But can she get the fire hot enough to roast it properly? She looks at the sun to tell the time. She must start now if the meal's to be ready in time. The woman stokes up the fire, opens the door so that the cottage doesn't get too hot and goes to look for some vegetables and some wild berries for dessert. Next year she hopes to plant some gooseberries and red currants. Then she can give her family a change from the apple pies she makes with fruit picked from her tree outside.

The hens start pecking at the door. The woman shoos them out and follows them to her little garden.

RESOURCEFUL ECONOMY 1871 to 1900

CPR TRANSFORMS THE PROVINCE

MINERS SWITCH TO COAL, SILVER, COPPER AND ZINC

FOREST GIANTS BUILD TOWNS

FISHING INDUSTRY GROWS

AROUND THE WORLD
AFRICA — 1871 Journalist John Stanley finds the missing explorer David Livingston
PANAMA — 1880 Work starts on the Panama Canal; it is not completed for 34 years
GERMANY — 1883 Otto Bismarck introduces health insurance for Germany

*POPULATION — 1901	
Native People	28,949 (16%)
British	106,403 (60%)
Other Europeans	21,784 (12%)
Asians	19,524 (11%)
Other	1,997 (1%)
Total	178,657

*ETHNIC ORIGIN

The gold rush of 1858 turned British Columbia into a colony. Union with Canada in 1871 made it a province. The coming of the railway in 1885 started the transition from a backwater into a modern industrial state.

Those 14 years between admission into Confederation and the driving of the last spike were anxious years for British Columbia's politicians and businessmen. They worried that Ottawa would renege its promise to start the railway in two years and be finished before ten. The economy was in tatters. Gold was no longer the mainspring of the economy, and the other industries—forestry, fishing and hard rock mining—were not yet strong enough to make up the loss. Everyone waited for the railway that would, they believed, bring settlers, goods and investment—and open up Canada and the eastern United States as a market for British Columbia.

Suffrage in B.C.:

The right to vote in both provincial and federal elections in B.C. was restricted by the political elite to suit its sexist, political, and racist needs. Women could not vote provincially until 1917, federally not until 1918. Native people and Chinese people officially lost the right to vote in 1874, the Japanese lost their right in 1895, and East Indian people in 1907. Provincial voting rights were restored slowly: Chinese and East Indians in 1947; native people and Japanese in 1949. Federal voting rights, which were either never granted or were taken away at various times, were given to all of these groups around the same time.

Political life in British Columbia at this time was as weak as the economy. The long tradition of B.C.'s politicians fighting Ottawa, rather than trying to solve their problems, got its start in the first years after joining Confederation. Finding enough intelligent persons who are willing to serve in politics is a universal problem. The needs of government often outstrip the supply of competent, well-educated, sensible—and willing—officials and politicians. British Columbia has never been free of this syndrome, especially so in the late nineteenth century. The European population numbered only about 9,000 and from this tiny group the province had to provide three senators and elect six members of Parliament and 25 members of the Legislature.

There were no political parties, just a continuum of shifting pressure groups which made it difficult for premiers to embark on any kind of program. In the first 32 years of democracy in British Columbia (1871-1903), 14 men served as premiers, the same number that have served since party politics in 1903.

The political elite of the province spent most of their time squabbling with Ottawa about the railway and about money. In spare moments, it stirred up arguments between those who lived on the mainland and those who liked life in Victoria and wanted to make certain that the long-awaited railway ended on their doorstep.

Building a railway through the Fraser Canyon was a daunting task. Tunnels and bridges dotted the track, clinging precariously to the rocky walls of the canyon. Heavy snowfalls often shut the track for weeks at a time.

As in the debate before joining Confederation, there were threats to secede. Concerned citizens signed petitions to Queen Victoria. They joined protests to persuade the visiting governor-general to meddle. There were reasons to be worried, it's true. Sir John A. Macdonald, the generous Conservative prime minister of the Confederation negotiations, left office in 1873 under a cloud of scandal. Surveys for the railway had started, but the Liberals did not share Macdonald's transcontinental dream. Their leader, Alexander Mackenzie, thought it was mad. And when the railway plans were revived in 1877, it became obvious that Ottawa favoured a route ending in an almost-deserted Burrard Inlet rather than one ending at Esquimalt, in the centre of British Columbia's most populated area.

But in September 1878, Sir John A. was re-elected to enact his so-called National Plan, with tariffs and the railway as its main thrusts. While Ottawa was still negotiating the final terms with the Canadian Pacific Railway Company, work began on the British Columbia section near Yale, in the Fraser Canyon, in May 1880. The contractor was Andrew Onderdonk, a 37-year-old American who was backed by a wealthy New York syndicate. He had lost his original bids on the various federal government contracts to build the line from Port Moody to Kamloops but, with Ottawa's connivance, had bought the contracts from lower bidders.

In addition to the massive land grants and a $25 million subsidy, Ottawa had also agreed to hand over to the CPR the line from Port Moody to Kamloops once it was built. Onderdonk, then, was building a railway which

Andrew Onderdonk (left), who supervised the building of the CPR from Port Moody to Eagle Pass, was 31 in 1880 when he, his wife and their four children came to live at Yale. From there he supervised the blasting, building and grading that took the track through the forbidding Fraser Canyon. Onderdonk—reserved, always polite and smartly dressed—was helped by his wife Delia (above), who entertained the notables who came to inspect his work. Delia also ran a small hospital for workers injured in accidents and explosions. Onderdonk—from a patrician New York family—was backed by a syndicate of wealthy bankers from New York and San Francisco. By 1883, he had run out of money and went to Ottawa to get help; he got none, but cut costs drastically by tightening the curves of the track and generally lowering standards. Onderdonk later built canals, tunnels and railways in Ontario, Argentina, Chicago and New York. Overwork killed him in 1905.

he would not have to operate. His cost-cutting measures—such as building numerous tight curves or forbidding gradients—might be good for a money-conscious contractor but they would make the running of trains through the canyon dangerous and expensive.

For the first year, Onderdonk blasted away up the canyon, maiming or killing hundreds as rocks fell and explosives caught fire. Since no track had been laid, Onderdonk had to move construction machinery, tools and food by mule and oxen teams over the trail built by Governor Douglas 20 years before. Costs were so high that Onderdonk decided in 1882 to build his own 250-ton river steamer, the *Skuzzy*. His plan: to sail her through Hell's Gate and its ten-knot current into a relatively calmer stretch upriver. Then he would use her to carry cargo and men between Boston Bar and Lytton. At first no skipper would take the *Skuzzy* through; those who tried nearly wrecked the ship. Onderdonk took charge. He ordered ring bolts driven into the canyon walls and ropes passed through them. A steam winch on board, helped by crewmen pulling on the capstan and a horde of Chinese labourers pulling perilously on shore, eventually pulled the *Skuzzy* through.

The Skuzzy *at work. The* Skuzzy *was the heroine of the battle of the Hells' Gate rapids. She was a typical small sternwheeler, 127 feet long with a 24-foot beam. She was built by Onderdonk's engineers at Tunnel City, near Spuzzum, about 20 miles upriver from Yale and a mile or so below Hell's Gate.*

Chinese labourers had helped build the American transcontinental. Since Onderdonk could not find enough white and native workmen—perhaps because his payscale ($1.75 a day) was less than that of American railroad contractors—he started to employ Chinese workers soon after he started work in 1880. They were paid only $1 a day, demanded no camps or cooks, and were less troublesome when work was done than the whites or natives.

British Columbians were horrified. After all, the Chinese not only looked different, they thought and acted differently and seemed a threat to civilisation as British Columbians knew it. To keep the Chinese out, a series of anti-Chinese laws and taxes was devised. Sometimes the immigrants fought back by going on strike for a couple of days. In 1882, Onderdonk brought in another 6,000 Chinese workers directly from China. Even with all this help, Onderdonk had only laid about 20 miles of track two years after he had started work—so difficult was the task of blasting and cutting a way along the side of the canyon.

Once Onderdonk's men had conquered the canyon, the going was relatively easy. By August 1885 they had gone past Kamloops and were building the line to Eagle Pass to link up with the mountain section being built by the railway. By October, Onderdonk's crews reached Eagle Pass and on the morning of November 7, the tracks were joined at a clearing in the forest called Craigellachie. The last spike was driven home. The workmen went back to their huts and camps to celebrate and to look for new jobs. The railway directors and contractors climbed into their train headed by a little wood-burning eight-wheeler which took them, in a happy mood, to Port Moody and the Pacific Ocean.

The winter shut down the transcontinental line in the

The Provincial and Federal governments introduced measures to reduce the Chinese population in B.C.:
1879-1880: petitions in B.C. Legislature demand ban on Chinese immigration.
1881: B.C. Legislature approves entry restrictions based on ability to write and speak English; the legislation was disallowed by Ottawa. Crowds met ships bringing Chinese immigrants to "persuade them to stay on board."
1885: Ottawa introduces head tax on Chinese. The amounts increased gradually, reaching $500 in 1903.
1897: Chinese workers were banned from B.C. public works projects.
1923: Ottawa bans all Chinese except diplomats.

Restrictions were relaxed in 1945, after the war. Groups today are fighting for retribution for the unjust head taxes paid almost a century ago.

THE INLAND SENTINEL

YALE, THURSDAY, MARCH 9, 1882

The C.P.R. Railway.
Another Powder Accid'nt.

Thompson River, Feb. 24, '82.
EDITOR SENTINEL:—A blow up occurred Wednesday morning at Camp 13, when Hugh Craig of San Francisco, was instantly killed and the following persons injured:
Thomas Williams injured in hands, head, eyes, one ear drum ruptured.
John Lawson badly cut in right arm.
John Dugan, who was standing only 15 ft. away, one eye slightly injured.
It is stated Craig went into Magazine at end of Tunnel No. 10 used for storing powder, to get 8 cases giant and 14 kegs black, when the explosion took place. Craig blown up against roof of Tunnel every bone in his body shattered—remains unrecognizable. Cause of explosion unknown.

—We devote large space in to-day's paper to the trials for selling liquor along the Railway line without Government license. The evidence discloses a terrible state of affairs upon our Public Works, and, we have reason to believe, the half is not yet told. No fault to the Government Officers here or Squire Pearson if a stop is not put to the violation of law and order. Mr. Onderdonk's occasional visits along the line have been missed of late, and the sooner he returns to Yale and up the Railway line the better for himself and partners in the contract. There is great need for a sharp look out.

Life in the construction camps: from the Inland Sentinel, *published in Emory, near Yale.*

The crowning moment—November 7, 1885: the track laid by Onderdonk's men meets the track from the Prairies, and the Last Spike is hammered home in a clearing called Craigellachie. Donald Smith, fur trader turned financier, does the honours. Craigellachie, miles from nowhere, is named after a rock in Banffshire, Scotland; CPR president George Stephen and Donald Smith both come from the area.

mountains. The first passenger train from Montreal did not arrive in Port Moody until July 4, 1886, after a journey of 139 hours. More than a thousand people greeted her. Nine miles to the west of the terminus, the railway's surveyors had already started to lay out the new townsite on the 6,000 acres they owned around the little settlement called Granville. They drove their first spike in the forest at what is now Victory Square and Vancouver was soon the ultimate company town, with the CPR's hand in almost every action, every deal. But the company did not want to stop in Vancouver. Out in the Pacific were more goods, more people. Three ocean-going ships, the *Abyssinia, Parthia* and *Batavia* were chartered in 1887 to carry freight (mostly tea and silk) and passengers from Yokohama, Shanghai and Hong Kong to the new port on the Pacific. Three gleaming white liners, the 6,000-ton *Empress of Japan, Empress of China* and *Empress of India* were ordered for service in 1891-2. The first of them, the *Empress of India,* docked in Vancouver on April 28, 1891, after a record 11-day run from Yokohama.

And, of course, passengers would need a first-rate hotel to stay in before and after they boarded trains and ships. Work started in July 1886 at the corner of Granville and

Georgia for the Hotel Vancouver. By the time it was finished, there would be no trouble finding your way there: on August 8, 1887, the Vancouver Electric Illumination Society (later, B.C. Electric, and still later, B.C. Hydro) started up its steam-powered generating plant at the corner of Abbott and Hastings. Three hundred street lights went on and the oil lamps were put away in 53 Vancouver homes.

The first Hotel Vancouver was on Granville Street, where Eaton's is now. It opened in May, 1887, a week before the first passenger train arrived. Granville was a new street and crews had just finished clearing the forest from the docks to False Creek. No-one could say that it was a beautiful building. And it had to be enlarged soon after being built. Few shops or offices came to keep the hotel company, though, and Cordova Street remained the main street until the turn of the century. Its successor, built a block away, was only half-finished when construction was stopped during the Depression.

The transcontinental railway's arrival in Vancouver meant that a much larger coastal shipping service was needed. More passengers and freight had to be carried to Vancouver Island and the Puget Sound area—and to the fishing and logging camps, canneries, mills and other settlements being built up the coast. The Hudson's Bay Company, which had provided coastal service for most of the century, had joined other firms in 1883 to form the

A clear sign that Vancouver was taking over from Victoria as the province's chief port was the arrival of the Abyssinia *on June 14, 1887. She was chartered by the CPR from the Cunard steamship line until the ships designed for the run—the Empresses—could take over the service in 1891.* Abyssinia *brought teas and silk (mostly for the London market), and some passengers.*

The CPR took over the coastal fleet of Canadian Pacific Navigation in 1901. A short time later, the Islander*—one of its prize passenger ships (shown here)—hit an iceberg near Skagway, Alaska—an area fatal to another CP liner,* Princess Sophia*, 17 years later. One of the CP Navigation ships taken over by the CPR was called* Princess Louise*; soon, most of the coastal fleet took Princess names to match the ocean fleet's Empresses.*

Canadian Pacific Navigation Company which took over a motley fleet of stern-wheelers and steamers of all sizes. Now, to handle the extra traffic from the CPR and the Great Northern, the company ordered the *Premier*, a 15-knot steamer with room for 300 passengers, from a San Francisco shipyard. She started service on August 5, 1887. A year later the Glasgow-built *Islander*, a 1,500-ton, 12-knot ship, also started service. But on August 15, 1901, just after the Canadian Pacific Railway had taken over the Canadian Pacific Navigation company, the *Islander* struck an iceberg near Skagway on her way to Vancouver and sank with 42 of her 172 passengers and crew. Union Steamships, formed in 1889, had divided the coastal trade with the CPN, leaving the Vancouver, Victoria, Seattle and Alaska trade to the larger company and serving, instead, the hundreds of smaller settlements.

East of Vancouver the railway built a branch line from Mission to provide a joint service with J.J. Hill's Great Northern in the U.S. But Hill was the villain in the southeastern corner of B.C. American prospectors from Idaho and Montana—looking for metals such as lead, copper, zinc, lode gold and silver—had spread into this region in the middle 1880s. Mining these metals demanded large amounts of capital for refineries—and a transportation system for the heavy loads of ore. Soon Nelson, Grand Forks, Sandon, New Denver, Rossland and Trail had grown into mining towns of world renown. Unfortunately for the CPR, Hill—a CPR director until 1883—was close at hand with his Great Northern line. The next few years was a time of blocked tracks, mergers, bluster, rate cutting, hurried building of spur lines, and fights between railwaymen as the railways fought for access and profits.

Then came the Crow's Nest Pass agreement with Ottawa in 1897, in which the CPR got a large subsidy for building a main line to the area through southern Alberta.

In return, the railway agreed to carry grain at fixed low rates. The opening of the Crow's Nest area created access to coal which until then had chiefly been mined around Nanaimo, on Vancouver Island. Here the chief customers, at first, were the Royal Navy's Pacific squadron and the steamships serving the Pacific coast. Demand grew as railway companies switched from wood to coal, and steam engines began to power sawmills, canneries and mines.

Sternwheelers were easily-built, adaptable ships of shallow draft that could be run ashore anywhere to land passengers and cargo. They sailed the rivers and lakes, particularly in south-eastern B.C., and filled in the gaps in the railway system.

The Hudson's Bay Company, first developers of the Nanaimo mines, had sold out to the Vancouver Coal and Land Company, which ran its mines in a paternalistic fashion. Its chief rival was a company run by a former Hudson's Bay Company mine manager, Robert Dunsmuir. He hired Chinese labourers and ran his mines with a grasping, brutal hand. A strike in 1877 had to be put down by the militia and the miners went back to work at greatly reduced pay. The Dunsmuir fortune was made even more secure when the Conservative government in Ottawa gave it a contract to build the Esquimalt-Nanaimo Railway in 1886; like the CPR, it got a massive subsidy and vast land grants. Dunsmuir and his son James (who succeeded his father in 1889) were in a virtual state of warfare with the miners for most of the rest of the century and the company's mines were deathtraps for miners.

When Sir John A. came to drive the Esquimalt and Nanaimo Railway's last spike on August 13, 1886 he was in want of a little nip to celebrate the occasion. It's said that Mrs. Dunsmuir refused to serve drinks and so Dunsmuir took the Prime Minister down one of his mineshafts; there they marked another triumph of Conservatism and capitalism.

The forest industry had grown enormously since the first small mills and logging camps started work near Victoria and Yale. Already in 1861 a New Westminster mill, powered by steam, was exporting dressed lumber to Australia and other markets. By the 1870s, two mills, served by six logging camps, were at work in Burrard Inlet. Four years before the CPR reached the coast, there were

Danger has always been the mate of coal miners and B.C.'s early coal mines had their share of disasters. Here, miners wait for news of their fellow workers after an explosion at the No. 1 Mine in Nanaimo in 1887.

more than 20 mills in the province. The railway not only increased demand for lumber for its own track and buildings, it also created new markets in the towns it fostered. Another market opened on the Prairies. The CPR also made vast tracts of forest accessible to logging and soon there was the familiar pattern of mergers, buy-outs and the creation of large corporations—chiefly financed by businessmen from eastern Canada. The new firms operated stores, hospitals, camps and tugboats and their own spur lines. Vast areas of provincial land were handed over to the forest companies as they demanded more and more raw timber for the mills.

Native people were barred from commercial fishing when B.C joined Confederation and Ottawa took over

Loggers and a donkey engine at Brown & Kirkland Logging Company, Pitt Lake. Logging has never been a trade for the weak or faint-hearted. In the late nineteenth century, it demanded a lot of hard work at the risk of injury due to falling trees or inexpertly handled axes.

native affairs. And so fishing (in small sailboats using gill nets) became essentially a white man's occupation until the first Japanese arrived in the late 1880s. But in the canneries that were being built in increasing numbers, the workers were a mixture of native people—mostly women—and Chinese. The fishing industry, chiefly directed to the export trade to Britain (about 60,000 cases of canned salmon went in 1877) was seasonal, working only two months of the year.

The first labour unions had been formed in British Columbia in the 1850s by immigrants from Britain working as bakers, shipbuilders and printers. But conditions were not ripe for the growth of unionism until the 1880s

Native women and Chinese men operated the fish-packing plants that produced cargoes like this in the 1880s and '90s. Canned salmon became the main dish of British working class Sunday teas. As in the lumber and mining industries, smaller plants were gobbled up until two giant firms dominated the industry for most of this century; now there is only one—B.C. Packers.

when the Knights of Labor, an early version of the Industrial Workers of the World, moved in from the United States. The Knights of Labor, however, was an industrial union, serving all the workers in a plant, not individual crafts. Since there were few large firms, it soon faded. But by the middle nineties there were more than 100 craft union locals in the province, representing painters, builders, masons, carpenters, longshoremen and railway workers. The fishermen's strike of 1900, when a hastily-formed group of militiamen had to be shipped to the mouth of the Fraser to protect the Japanese fishermen who carried on working, showed that militant unions were now a part of British Columbia's industrial society. The growth of the union movement spurred the growth of political parties, and so political life changed, too.

The first Japanese people came to Victoria in 1877, but serious immigration from Japan did not begin until the1890s. The first Japanese worked as fishermen around Steveston, like the man shown here. Others went to farms in the Fraser Valley and Okanagan.

As settlement and industry grew, the native people were pushed more and more out of the mainstream of life in B.C. The industries which suited their skills, like trapping and fishing, either faded or were denied them. In the other industries—forestry, fish canning and mining—they had to compete with better-positioned Europeans or the Chinese. The missionaries increased their work, usually well-meant but often destructive. Disease and despair were the native peoples' constant companions. In 1871, there were 26,000 natives out of a total population of 36,000. By 1901, 29,000 native people competed with 179,000 Europeans and Asians. By 1911, there were only 20,000 native people left.

Empress of India arrives at Victoria

FROM OUR CORRESPONDENT
Tuesday, April 28, 1891

VICTORIA— At six o'clock this morning the citizens of this capital city were awakened by the fire bell's striking 12 times. They dressed in their finest and walked and drove to the Outer Wharf in the hundreds to see the *Empress of India* lying about half a mile off. Her white hull gleamed through the morning mist and from stem to stern she was festooned with bunting to celebrate her arrival after a record run from Yokohama, in the Japanese Islands. The liner is the first of the three new Canadian Pacific ships which will call at Victoria after a voyage across the Pacific from the Orient. The "White Empresses," as some wags are already calling them, have twin engines and propellors and steam at around 15 knots, with a maximum of 19 knots—sufficient to bring the *Empress of India* from Yokohama in 10 days, 11 hours and 36 minutes. One of her precedessors, the *Abyssinia,* took just more than 14 days. If the *Empress of India* is any indication, the ships are magnificent tributes to British shipbuilding and to the Canadian Pacific Railway's determination to preserve its rightfully-deserved command of the passenger and cargo trade across the Pacific, an ocean which is also the domain of American ships serving Seattle and San Francisco.

There was a festive mood befitting the occasion, as the invited guests and medical and customs officials went out on the *Lorne* and *Pilot* to board the ocean greyhound, which has a tonnage of

Empress of India, *the pride of the CPR, steams past Stanley Park and the wreck of the 55-year old paddle steamer, the* Beaver.

5,940. One local businessman—who claimed he was versed in the details of the shipping and railway business—was heard to tell anyone who would listen that the old ships chartered by the company, such as the *Abyssinia,* made enough money to save the Canadian Pacific Railway from trouble in the current business decline. The new ships, the *Empress of China, Empress of Japan* and the *Empress of India,* would be the future saviours of the company in these difficult times, he believed. He pointed out that all the old ships took only about 280 saloon passengers a year. The new ships would carry close to 1,000 a year, and that was in addition to their cargoes of silk, tea and opium, and steerage passengers.

After a tour of the ship, with its gleaming staterooms, dining saloon, smoking room and library, the visitors assembled in the dining saloon where Mayor Grant praised the seamanship of Captain O. Marshall and presented the popular captain of the ship with a silver punch bowl and cups, made especially for the occasion and bearing a suitable inscription.

The 131 passengers on board also had nothing but good words for the captain and crew. One hundred of them had boarded the liner for this, her first voyage, when she left Liverpool, England, on February 8. They had paid $600 for a "world cruise" and had docked at Gibraltar, Marseilles, Naples, Suez, Colombo, Penang, Singapore, Hong Kong, Kobe and Nagasaki before crossing the Pacific from Yokohama. The passengers, consisting of families and single men, some travelling with their valets, said that the weather was mostly fine but the ship had passed through a cyclone eight days ago. One passenger, a retired Royal Navy captain, said the liner rolled badly in rough seas and that she needed some stabilisers to handle bad weather. He said he was going to write to officials of the company to complain when he got back to London.

The promenade deck of the Empress of India. *There was little space for passengers and recreation on the first Pacific liners. Cabins were small, and facilities were shared.*

Breakfast was served by the crew to passengers and guests at eight o'clock and soon afterwards the guests left on the *Lorne* and the *Pilot;* the *Empress of India* sailed for Vancouver at 9:45. Pilot Urquhart was on the bridge and the gleaming white ocean greyhound took the Outside Channel on her short voyage to Vancouver. Her estimated time of arrival in that city was set for 2:50 this afternoon.

Empress of India attempts record journey

FROM OUR CORRESPONDENT
Tuesday, April 28, 1891

VANCOUVER—Just before two o'clock today, when the *Empress of India* was due to arrive in Vancouver, businessmen, workers and women with their children left their offices and homes and started to walk down Granville and the surrounding streets towards the Canadian Pacific Railway's wharf. Despite the heavy rain, some bold citizens climbed onto roofs to get a better view. The assembled crowd waited patiently until just before three o'clock, when a gun was fired from the lookout and the white prow of the liner, like the figurehead of a sailing-ship, could be seen through a clump of trees at Brockton Point. The City Band struck up and played on as the *Empress of India* slowly moved towards the wharf close to the Canadian Pacific Railway station on Cordova. She presented a splendid sight with her

The first White Empress arrives at Vancouver's CPR dock. Most offices and homes are deserted as the crowd braves the rain to greet the ship.

many-coloured streamers fluttering in the breeze and her lady passengers in their handsome clothes lining the rails. Loud expressions of admiration were heard from all around and, as the first line was thrown, all the passengers and crew, joined by the crowd on shore, gave three hearty cheers.

Mr. Cornelius Van Horne, President of the Canadian Pacific Railway, had been waiting in his official Pullman cars; he was the first person to step onto the ship. Soon after he briskly went up the gangplank, he was followed by Mayor Oppenheimer, the aldermen of the city, and members of the Board of Trade. Mr. Van Horne was conducted round the ship by Captain Marshall and inspected her thoroughly. He was heard to express his approval of the ship, her officers and crew. Some aldermen who went through the ship, however, were concerned at the size of her holds for steerage passengers and told the Mayor they feared that more large numbers of Chinese, Japanese and East Indians would soon be flocking into Vancouver.

Captain O. Marshall, master of the Empress of India. *After his service with the CPR, he was honoured by an appointment to Trinity House, helping to run Britain's lighthouses.*

The passengers had by this time landed, and those who were to stay in Vancouver had registered in their hotels while those continuing their journey disembarked straight into the special train waiting at the station. Consisting of two Pullman cars, two official cars, a baggage car and an observation car, the train left the Canadian Pacific Railway station at 6:10 pm and will go through as fast as possible to try to establish a record of 21 days for the journey from Yokohama to London.

Before the special train left, Mayor Oppenheimer presented an illuminating address to Mr. Van Horne in his official car. The Mayor said that he and the city were proud to be celebrating the completion of that great international chain which the perseverance and energy of the Canadian people had forged to connect the Mother Country with the Orient. This chain provided a rapid and complete service of communication with which no other nation could present an equal. He said that the citizens of Vancouver were under a deep obligation to Mr. Van Horne who was the head of that magnificent corporation whose coming had called Vancouver into being. The arrival of this splendid steamer marked the coming of age of Vancouver as a seaport and gave it the right to assume its position as one of the centres of maritime commerce.

This evening a banquet and dance will be held in the Hotel Vancouver. Many of the ladies of society are looking forward to meeting Mr. Van Horne. They will be grievously disappointed; Mr. Van Horne is not a sociable man and detests small talk, especially of the female variety, and left Vancouver on the special train.

BOOM, BUST, BANG-BANG 1900 - 1950

New Kind of Premier—New Kind of Politics

Prosperity—Then Mind-Numbing Depression

Two World Wars Topple Old Order

Women Get The Vote—and Welding Rods

AROUND THE WORLD
United States — 1903 Orville and Wilbur Wright fly their biplane for 57 seconds
Russia — 1917 Bolsheviks led by Trotsky storm Winter Palace in Petrograd
Japan — 1945 First atomic bomb destroys Hiroshima; 101,000 people are killed

*POPULATION — 1941	
Native People	24,882 (3%)
British	571,336 (70%)
Other Europeans	175,512 (21.5%)
Asians	42,472 (5%)
Other	3,659 (.5%)
Total	817,861

*ETHNIC ORIGIN

The events which had shaped British Columbia until 1901—European exploration, the gold rush, joining Confederation, the arrival of the CPR—were benign. The events which shaped the next 40 years were malignant—outbursts of racism, two wars and a shattering Depression. Since few people are cursed with a vision of the future, however, the people of British Columbia saw the turn of the century as a time of increasing optimism: more jobs, more investment, more money and better politics.

The squabbling in a system uncontrolled by party discipline had meant that since 1871 local, petty issues had dominated the Legislature, made its policies inconsistent and left it open to manipulation by powerful groups. The advent of party politics in 1903 did not mean that suddenly all the bickering and manipulation stopped. It did mean, however, that local pressures on legislators, and in particular on premiers, could be diverted by

A mule train waits patiently outside a store selling supplies for Klondike miners on Vancouver's Cordova Street in 1898. Perhaps the mules were there to carry purchases to the docks nearby. It's more likely, however, that they were part of the store's sales campaign. The gold rush trade helped to push Vancouver ahead of Victoria as a business centre. Money flowed into the city and property values climbed. A lot which sold for $100 in 1887 when the first CPR train arrived was worth $100,000 in 1912. Population in 1892 was 15,000; in 1905, it reached 45,000; in 1910, it had climbed to 98,000.

claiming that the party's interests lay elsewhere. And party discipline meant that longer-term policies could be engaged without fear of immediate defeat.

Another cause for optimism: after two decades of indifferent political leadership, a bright, young New Westminster lawyer, Richard McBride, became Conservative premier in June 1903. Energetic and intelligent, McBride believed that transportation and an open door for investment were the keys to prosperity in a province so dependent on resources. But first, there was the usual demand to Ottawa for more money. Ottawa claimed that the provincial taxes were too low and suggested that McBride raise them.

There was no shortage of money coming into the province. Americans, Britons and some Europeans believed, like the investors from Hong Kong and Japan 80 years later, that British Columbia was a safe and relatively profitable place for their money. The depression of the the last half of the decade was fading away, helped by the Klondike gold rush of 1898, when boarding houses and ships to the north were full and stores supplying the miners and prospectors were busy all day.

American investors and entrepreneurs dominated the timber industry. The demand caused by the building of railways and the growth of new towns across the American West had stripped Minnesota and Wisconsin of their timber stands. But President Teddy Roosevelt, the energetic outdoorsman who had come to the White House in 1901, was determined to save the forests and mountains of the United States from the profiteers. In the next few years he put 148,000,000 acres into National Forests. Over the border, however, there was a government dedicated to creating prosperity and not at all worried about the forests and mountains. If firms would agree to operate a sawmill,

J.W. Horne's real estate office in a hollow log at Georgia and Granville, 1886.

There was no mistaking the purpose of life in Vancouver in the early 1900s: in 1908 real estate firms outnumbered grocery stores three to one. British historian J.A.Hobson on the city:

"It is a purely business town, a thing of stores and banks and meagre wooden houses, with no public buildings of account.... The stranger is amazed at the profusion of solid banking houses; it would almost seem as if the inhabitants must be a race of financiers, concerned purely with money and stocks and shares."

Victoria would give them 21-year leases of timber for very small rents. In two years after 1901, nearly 15,000 licences had been issued. Fortunes were made by speculators and the foundations of the large forest empires were laid.

Men such as the American Peter Larson combined railway building with logging and land speculation. Well before the Grand Trunk Pacific had decided on Prince Rupert as its terminus, he bought the land on which Prince Rupert stands. One of his associates was another American, J.H. Bloedel, soon to be a famous name in provincial forests. Through

H.R. MacMillan, who created Canada's largest forest company, was born in Ontario in September 1885, and came to work in B.C.'s forests in 1907. In 1912, he headed the province's forest service. He travelled around the world during the First World War trying to sell B.C. softwood; his report on the trip was ignored and in 1919, backed by British money, he started his own lumber export business. To ensure supply, he bought his own mills and, by purchases and mergers, he built the giant MacMillan Bloedel company. He died in Vancouver in 1976.

Alvo Von Alvensleben was one of the exotic investors who has made B.C.'s financial life so intriguing. His family invested heavily in the lumber industry and in real estate; they built the Dominion Trust tower at Cambie and Hastings in Vancouver in 1908. The family was said to be an agent of the Imperial German Army, even of the Kaiser himself. When war erupted, Von Alvensleben was interned.

marriage, friendship and business association, a small group of Americans became giants of the forests bringing money, management skills and the latest techniques. Just before the First World War, there were 400 sawmills and more than 800 logging camps at work in the province, and forestry firms paid more than $2,300,000 a year in fees and royalties. Company towns sprung up as some of the firms started to operate mills far from cities but close to water and trees.

Not all the trees in B.C.'s forests were cut to make planks and posts. The demand for wood pulp to make paper to feed the presses of North America, Europe and Japan had prompted the building of pulp mills in eastern Canada in the 1870s. The first attempts to build pulp mills in B.C. came at the turn of the century but the first successful mill did not start operating until 1909 at Swanson Bay on Vancouver Island. Soon other plants were in operation at Ocean Falls and Powell River, and in April 1912 the *Vancouver Daily Province* started using Powell River newsprint.

When war came in 1914, the export trade collapsed and domestic demand fell dramatically. But German submarines sank so many Allied ships that a crash wooden-ship-building program was started in 1917. Since about 1,500,000 board feet of first-rate lumber was needed for each ship, special logging camps and sawmills opened and most loggers were working again. Another crash program sent more loggers to work in the Queen Charlottes cutting spruce so that the aircraft factories of Europe could build Sopwith Camels, SE5s, Spads and the other planes for the Billy Bishops of the Allied air forces.

After the war, the industry continued rationalisation and turned its energies to marketing. Selling agencies were formed, one in 1919 by H.R. MacMillan, chief provincial forester and federal timber trade commissioner. The company expanded into the shipping business and soon owned

The end of the 19th century saw the creation of company towns built around mills and mines. The employer owned the townsite, the homes, stores, and occasionally even the churches. The new massive machinery was only economic when processing supplies of raw materials that would last for decades; large industrial complexes were built close to raw materials and water but far from cities and a steady supply of workers. The employers' solution was to hire workers to live in towns built near their work and provide them with all the comforts of a city. Once hired and settled down miles from anywhere, however, workers often found they were only a little better than modern-day slaves, dependent on the employer for virtually everything.

its own mills and camps. By the late twenties the industry was setting production and profitability records. Then the Depression cut output in the province's mills to the lowest mark since 1869. By 1938, however, an active selling campaign had put the industry back to work. When war came again in 1939, the industry came under government control and prospered, largely because the British market was cut off from its Scandinavian suppiers.

Similar patterns governed the development of the two other major industries of the province—fishing and mining. British money financed mergers and the formation of big fish-packing firms. They started to run their own fishing fleets and built docks and harbours so that larger fishboats could bring in their catches. The boats dropped their sails and installed simple gasoline engines. This meant they could go further afield for more species and enjoy a longer season. Purse seine nets and trolling added to their catches. In the canneries, machinery such as the "iron chink" cut and cleaned the fish and meant that 25 workers could do 100 persons' work.

The hard-rock mining industry was largely controlled by American investors. They improved techniques and machinery to meet the demands from the new industries of the American middle west, such as the automobile

Work in the fish canneries was usually divided on sexist and racist lines. Chinese men gutted and cut the fish; Native women trimmed and canned it. The invention in 1900 of a mechanical gutter, with its steel belly filled with knives and brushes, and nicknamed the "iron chink," cut the Chinese cannery work force drastically.

By the 1920's, there was virtually no room for any new industrial plants in Vancouver, or so city-boosters pointed out as they tried to shuck off its image as a frontier town, only interested in lumber and fish. More than 1,000 industrial plants were operating with 27,000 workers producing $100 million worth of goods a year. Fifty steamship lines used the docks. Foundries, steel works, pulp and paper plants, printing, ship-building—these were just a few of Vancouver's industries. The boosters did not mention that only 8% of the industrial products were not linked to resource industries—a figure that is still close to today's.

factories of Henry Ford and Walter Chrysler.

As industries grew, the significance of agriculture in the economy dwindled. Gradually the arable parts of the province were bought, cleared, cultivated and brought into production with emphasis on supplying the growing cities and suburbs with milk, fresh vegetables and fruit. Most food, however, was imported. Ranchers started running cattle on the dry land around Kamloops and in the Cariboo.

Immigrants and investors, attracted by the climate of the Okanagan and the potential of the land once it was irrigated, flowed into the area. Some immigrants were seeking to recreate Edwardian England, just as the first settlers tried to establish mid-century England around Victoria. Other genteel immigrants, younger sons who had little chance of inheriting the family estate, joined companies which bought land and then tried to turn it into English-style villages.

If one railway—the CPR—had made money and brought prosperity to British Columbia, then more railways would bring even more money and more prosperity. That's the way the thinking went. Research into potential demand and rigorous costing were not wanted. If there were generous governments and foolish investors then it was time to build a railway.

There were to be two more transcontinental railways. One, the Grand Trunk Pacific, was to extend from Winnipeg across northern Manitoba, Saskatchewan, Alberta and British Columbia to Prince Rupert. It was incorporated in 1903 and built in eight years, from 1906 to 1914.

The first Grand Trunk Pacific train steams into Prince Rupert from Winnipeg—April 9, 1914.

The early 20th century was B.C.'s boom time for railways. Two were national and short-lived—the Grand Trunk Pacific and the Canadian Northern. The Pacific Great Eastern, now BC Rail, is alive and well in the B.C. Interior.

For Premier Richard McBride, provincial support of the Canadian Northern Pacific was fine but not enough. In 1912, he authorised provincial bonds to finance the building of the Pacific Great Eastern railway that would link Burrard Inlet with the northern Interior and the Canadian Northern line. But construction was bedeviled by scandal, and critics said the railway was merely a disguised Tory campaign fund. Only parts of the line (North Vancouver to Horseshoe Bay and Squamish to Clinton) were built when the government took over in 1919.

It never made money and dragged down its parent firm, the Grand Trunk Railway, which had operated in Quebec and Ontario since 1852. The GTP was taken over by the federal government in 1919 and incorporated into the Canadian National in 1923.

William Mackenzie and Donald Mann were the promoters of the second railway—the Canadian Northern Pacific. They persuaded Premier Richard McBride to sign a contract with them without the approval of his Cabinet on October 9, 1909. McBride offered financial help and massive land grants and was so generous that Mackenzie and Mann used the spare cash to buy a large coal company. The Canadian Northern's route crossed the Prairies and then used the Yellowhead Pass rejected by the CPR. Then it ran down the Fraser Canyon, usually on the other side of the river from the CPR. The last spike was driven at Ashcroft in the summer of 1915, and the first train arrived

Union Membership
Percentage of work force:
1911 — 12%
1919 — 22%
1934 — 7%
1939 — 14%
1945 — 30%
1958 — 55%
1970 — 49%
1980 — 43%
1991 — 38%
Note: agricultural workers are not included in these figures.

in Vancouver in October using Great Northern tracks. Like the Grand Trunk Pacific, the Canadian Northern's construction was a sad tale of blunders and financial chicanery, but government purses had run dry and the line was bankrupt before it reached Vancouver. The Canadian Northern, too, was folded into Canadian National in 1923.

The growth of big business led to the growth of big unions. Militant labour groups such as the Industrial Workers of the World (Wobblies) came in from the United States before the 1914 war and formed branches here. They attracted railwaymen, miners and other workers in industries where wages and conditions were bad. The Wobblies regarded political action as valueless and placed more emphasis on demonstrations and strikes. There was no shortage of targets for them. Thousands of workers were demanding better pay and conditions. In 1910, there were strikes in mines, the fishing industry, and the construction gangs building the Grand Trunk Pacific and Canadian Northern railways. More work stoppages plagued the construction of the Grand Trunk Pacific's terminus at Prince Rupert in 1911, and sailors from the Royal Canadian Navy were called in to restore order. A strike in 1911 involving the labourers building the Canadian Northern's tracks down the Fraser Canyon was put down harshly and strike leaders were given stiff sentences. And in 1913 coal miners at Cumberland, near Nanaimo, went on strike. Japanese and Chinese workers were brought in and the strikers rioted in Nanaimo, wrecking buildings and terrorising the town. Militiamen were called in to help the police

Albert 'Ginger' Goodwin—a labour organizer—was shot by police outside Cumberland on July 27, 1918. He was 31. On August 2, the day of his funeral, union members in Vancouver started a 24-hour general strike and fought with returning servicemen. Goodwin's friends maintained that he had been gunned down, not because he had tried to avoid arrest and military service, but because of his record as a strike-leader in the Kootenays.

and stayed on guard until war broke out in August 1914.

In Vancouver in 1918 high, uncontrolled food prices were the reason for stoppages involving longshoremen, streetcar workers and city employees. On August 2 there was a massive strike in Vancouver to protest the killing of Albert "Ginger" Goodwin, a union organiser wanted for evading conscription. Servicemen just back from France started a counter-protest and jumped on streetcars to force drivers to stay on the streets and not go back to the depot.

The Depression crushed the labour movement so that in 1934 only seven per cent of the workers were in unions. But as the war came and factories opened again, union membership increased and reached 30 per cent in the middle of the war. Workers' associations such as the Trades and Labour Congress and Canadian Congress of Labour grew more powerful and started recruitment drives in agriculture and service industries.

British Columbia's political culture was formed in the first quarter of the century. The Conservatives and Liberals viewed the creation of wealth as all-important, and in the first 25 years they made certain that entrepreneurs lacked nothing. Land, financial help, benign legislation and the use of the police or the military to control workers when necessary—all of these were handed out by the government, so long as jobs were created and investors got dividends. Naturally, this kind of politics caused an equal and opposite reaction. Since the thirties, labour unions, reform movements and parties promoting greater power for the state and a gentler society have challenged the old-line alliances in a seemingly perpetual polarisation.

Richard McBride, the first Conservative premier, was an extrovert, a glad-hander who toured the province and exuded optimism. He was helped at first by a booming economy and the fad for railways. But by 1914 his railway deals were duds. The economy slowed down and his vision lost its gleam. Ill with a disabling kidney disease, McBride resigned in 1915 and went to London as a special envoy to help the war effort. He died soon after he arrived there. McBride's successor had the unfortunate name of Bowser and lasted less than a year. By 1916, a 60-30 split of the popular vote for the Tories had become a 50-40 split for the Liberals and they took power. But their new leader,

Party Politics

Before 1903 no party system existed. Premiers depended on the support of changing coalitions.

Date	***Premier/Party***
1903	*McBride/Cons**
1915	*Bowser/Cons*
1916	*Brewster/Lib*
1918	*Oliver/Lib*
1927	*MacLean/Lib*
1928	*Tolmie/Cons*
1933	*Pattullo/Lib*
1941	*Hart/Lib-PC*
1947	*Johnson/Lib-PC*
1952	*Bennett/Socred*
1972	*Barrett/NDP***
1975	*Bennett/Socred*
1986	*Vander Zalm/Socred*
1991	*Johnston/Socred*
1991	*Harcourt/NDP*

**Conservatives became Progressive Conservatives in 1942.*

***CCF became New Democratic Party in 1961.*

The Popular Vote

Until 1933 Conservatives and Liberals split about 90% of the popular vote. In 1933 the CCF Opposition won 32% to Pattullo's 42. Since then the CCF/NDP Opposition vote has ranged from 46% (1979) to 28% (1956). Socreds won .4% in 1949 but increased their rate to 30% in 1952—enough to gain more seats than the CCF which had a 34% popular vote. Barrett won with 40% in 1972 and lost with 39% in 1975. Harcourt's NDP won with 42% in 1991, down from 43% in 1986 and 45% in 1983.

Harlan Brewster, died after less than two years in the premier's office and was succeeded in 1918 by a colleague, John Oliver.

Oliver was a political backroom man's dream. He had worked in the coal mines in England, come to Canada, taken various jobs, and then become an honest man of the soil, running a successful pig farm in Delta. Where McBride had a vision of railways, "Honest John" had a vision of dirt and ditches. Convinced that agriculture was the key to the province's prosperity, he drained Sumas Prairie and irrigated large tracts of the Okanagan. More large tracts of land in the Peace River were sold to would-be farmers. But cancer killed Oliver in 1927 and his successor John MacLean, another unknown, lasted a year.

It was the Tories' turn again. Simon Fraser Tolmie—is there a better name for a B.C. politician?—was the new premier. An Ottawa organiser for the Conservatives, he had come to British Columbia to help the provincial party select a new leader. None could be found, so Tolmie got the job. The Depression was the death of better politicians than Tolmie and he showed little understanding of the catastrophe that had struck the province.

Premier Thomas Dufferin (Duff) Pattullo woos a future voter. Patullo, Liberal premier from 1933 to 1941, lived a long, exciting life. He was born in 1873 and was a newspaperman in Ontario before he went to the Yukon and served as a government administrator until 1902. Pattullo then became a businessman in Dawson City and, later, in Prince Rupert. Elected to the Legislature in 1916, he became Minister of Lands. After a spell in Opposition, he became premier in the middle of the Depression. Pattullo died in 1956.

In the 1933 election the reaction was obvious. Liberal Duff Pattullo, an admirer of President Roosevelt's New Deal policies, became premier with 42% of the popular vote. The Conservatives disappeared in a flurry of splinter parties, and the Cooperative Commonwealth Federation got 32%—but only seven seats to Pattullo's 34. Pattullo tried to improve welfare payments, started agricultural stabilisation boards, built bridges and improved the lot of the poor and jobless. But his left-wing opponents accused him of trying to put a smile on the face of capitalism. He did little for the unemployed and homeless, they said, forgetting that Pattullo's powers were limited and that Ottawa

Helen Gregory MacGill (1864 to 1947)—journalist, feminist, mother, and judge—was the first woman to graduate from Trinity College, Toronto. She became a journalist and foreign correspondent. In 1903 she came to Vancouver and in 1917 was named the first woman judge in Western Canada. For most of her life she fought eagerly for reform to the status of women and for more sympathetic treatment of children. Her daughter, Elizabeth, was the first woman graduate in electrical engineering at University of Toronto, and became an aeronautical engineer, designer of the Maple Leaf training plane.

took refuge in doing nothing.

By 1937, the Conservatives had formed lines again and were challenging the CCF as the opposition. Pattullo won the election but should have seen the crisis coming. In 1941, the CCF increased its popular vote by five per cent to 34 per cent. The Liberals got 33 and the Tories 31. Right-wing Liberals, concerned at the left-wing surge, joined with the Conservatives and kicked Pattullo out. New Liberal leader John Hart became head of a coalition government that stayed in power—with different leaders—until the 1950s.

Theatres quickly opened up in the prosperous, brash city of Vancouver. The Opera House, next to the Hotel Vancouver, opened in 1891 with the backing of the CPR. The Pantages Theatre featured plays, musicals, vaudeville, and finally, movies.

When they weren't coping with wars, economic slumps, strikes and the chicanery and stupidity of their politicians, British Columbians found time to enjoy themselves. Vancouver's first theatre, Hart's Opera House, had opened in 1887 on Carrall Street and in a couple of years there were ten more. Others entertained crowds in Victoria and the Kootenay towns. Straight

Rum Runners

A few days after Prohibition became law in the U.S., enterprising B.C. seamen converted boats to take Canadian-distilled booze across Juan de Fuca Strait and down the coast. They were workers in a miniature market system run by dealers who set up depots, sold to other dealers and organised delivery runs. Dealers paid smugglers $11.00 a case; a small fishboat could carry 75 cases.

Slower boats would leave their B.C. depots in late morning so their run through U.S. waters was in the dark. Other specially-built boats sported Packard and Fiat aero-engines and could easily outrun U.S. Coast Guard boats in daylight. But danger came from hijackers, not the Coast Guard. In September 1924, a small depot ship, the Beryl G., *was ransacked and sunk off Sidney Island; her crew, William Gillis and his son, were killed. In January 1926, two men were hanged for the murders at Oakalla prison, near Vancouver.*

plays and musicals were on the bills at first; then came vaudeville companies with stars such as Charlie Chaplin and Stan Laurel. Polish pianist, and later president, Ignace Paderewski played at the Opera House. Diaghilev's Ballet Russe, with Nijinsky as the star, entertained Vancouver's elite on January 15, 1917. In 1905 some theatres added a moving picture to the bill, and gradually the movies pushed the live actors off stage. Jazz and, later, swing bands played for dancers in hotel ballrooms and clubs.

On Sundays the churches and their Sunday schools dictated most families' activities and tried to lay a veneer of gentility over the harshness of life in a still immature province. Bars were everywhere and brothels were tucked away discreetly in selected districts. The brothels were not talked about in society but drinking was, and reform movements—led by the churches and women's groups—attacked the problems caused by cheap and easily obtainable beer and spirits. In 1916 women celebrated a double victory: bars and booze were outlawed, and women were given the provincial vote. (women won the federal vote in 1918). But the bars opened again in 1921 and the government took over the sale of liquor.

Just over the border, drinkers were not so fortunate and distillers and distributors working in the province made fortunes as they sold hootch to the thirsty Americans. Coal Harbour in Vancouver and the Gulf Islands were the home bases of the rum-running trade as speedboats supplied the northern Pacific coast and mother ships with tenders tried to satisfy thirsty Californians. Other adventurers drove big cars loaded with liquor over the border.

This was the time when newspapers flourished on competition. In Victoria, the *British Colonist* and the *Victoria Times* had been informing and cajolling the people of the capital for 50 years or more. In New Westminster, John Robson, an ardent Confederationist and later premier, had founded the *British Columbian* at around the same time. The newspaper trade in Vancouver, following the patterns of the forestry and fishing industries, saw mergers, buy-outs and bankruptcies as the *Advertiser, News Advertiser, World, Daily Province, Telegram, Sun, Star* and *News Herald* jostled for business. In the 1920s the two strongest newspapers, the *Sun* and *Daily*

THE VANCOUVER SUN

"The People's Paper"

The Sun Is the Only Evening Paper Owned, Controlled and Operated by Vancouver Men

ESTABLISHED 1888 VOL. LXXIII—NO. 229 | 2¢ PER COPY | VANCOUVER, B.C., MONDAY, MARCH 12, 1928 | VANCOUVER, BY-MILE TRADING AREA, 562,675 GREATER VANCOUVER, POPULATION, 917,100

B.C. Over-spent $140,000 On One University Building

RAILWAY BOARD HEAD TO BE LT.-GOVERNOR?

OTTAWA—Lorem ipsum dolor sit amet, consectetur adipiscing elit, sed diam nonummy nibh euismod tincidunt ut laoreet dolore aliquam erat volutpat. [illegible]

Ryan and Palmer Jobs Under Fire in the Legislature

Government Witnesses Claim There Was Big Saving

VICTORIA, March 5— Just before public the public accounts committee adjourned the statement was made that the architect firm of Sharpe & Thompson had been paid to date $113,000 in fees on the University buildings at Point Grey.

VICTORIA—Lorem ipsum dolor sit amet, consectetur adipiscing elit, sed diam nonummy nibh euismod tincidunt ut laoreet dolore aliquam erat volutpat. [illegible]

House to Vote As a Unit for Oriental Ban

Liberal Member Will Introduce Resolution as Compromise.

VICTORIA—Lorem ipsum dolor sit amet, consectetur adipiscing elit, sed diam nonummy nibh euismod tincidunt ut laoreet dolore aliquam erat volutpat. [illegible]

GAMING HOUSE FINES BOOSTED

Magistrate Shaw increased the usual fine of $50 imposed in cases of keeping a gaming house. Lorem ipsum dolor sit amet, consectetur adipiscing elit, sed diam nonummy nibh euismod tincidunt ut laoreet dolore aliquam erat volutpat. [illegible]

PUZZLE: DEFINE WOMAN!

Is She 'Person' or Not; Supreme Court Will Decide

Vancouver's newspapers fought for scoops and readers in the '20s.

Province competed for readers and advertisements in ways that made Vancouver an exciting town for both readers and journalists.

So far this has been a story about making money, enjoyment, fighting for political power and raising families—acceptable things. Now it becomes a story about the underside—racism, wars and the Depression.

British Columbia at the turn of the century was a Little England. The attitude among those from Britain was that the best immigrants came from the Old Country. Americans

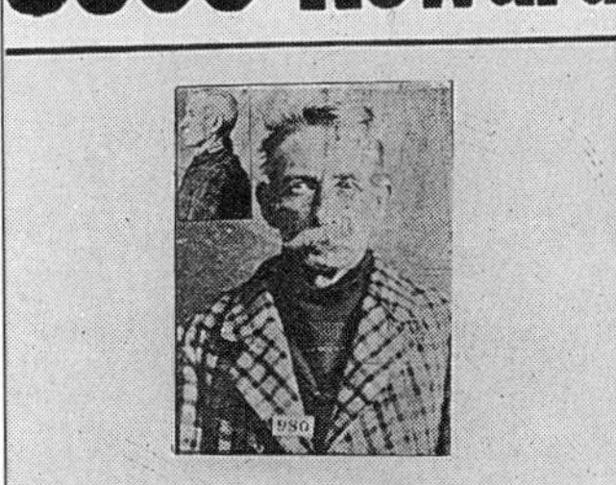

$500 Reward

The above reward will be paid for the arrest and detention of WILLIAM (Bill) MINER, alias Edwards, who escaped from the New Westminster Penitentiary at New Westminster, British Columbia, on the 8th August, 1907, where he was serving a life sentence for train robbery.

DESCRIPTION:

Age 65 years; 138 pounds; 5 feet 8½ inches; dark complexion; brown eyes; grey hair; slight build; face spotted; tattoo base of left thumb, star and ballet girl right forearm; wrist joint-bones large; moles centre of breast, 1 under left breast, 1 on right shoulder, 1 on left shoulder-blade; discoloration left buttock; scars on left shin, right leg, inside, at knee, 2 on neck.

Communicate with

Newspaper accounts of crime enlivened drab lives. On September 10, 1904, Bill Miner—just released from San Quentin Prison in the U.S.—held up a CPR transcontinental train near Mission and escaped with cash by rowing across the Fraser. Less than two years later, on May 14, 1906, Miner held up another train but was chased by a posse and captured near Kamloops. He was sentenced to 25 years in New Westminster Penitentiary; he escaped in August 1907 and fled to the States, where he died in 1913.

The Wah Chong family laundry in Vancouver in 1884. Despite discrimination and violence, the tightly-knit Chinese community survived and prospered.

ranked next and then other Europeans. People whose skins were not white and who worshipped different gods were beyond the pale.

The first Chinese had come to British Columbia with John Meares in 1788 but did not stay. In 1858 some Chinese from the United States joined the gold rush and then settled. They were joined by large numbers in the 1880s as the railways made deals with Chinese contractors to import cheap labour. When railway work finished the Chinese became shopkeepers, farmers, servants and laundrymen and set up Chinese settlements in the towns. The first Japanese man came in 1878. Others followed in the early 1880s and worked in sawmills, on farms and, a little later, as fishermen. They, too, stayed, started families and formed their own settlements such as at Steveston on the Fraser and on Powell Street in Vancouver. Sikhs also started coming in the 1880s as the shipping service between the Orient and Vancouver began. Back home they were loggers and farmers, and they worked in British Columbia in the same trades.

All these groups came to British Columbia seeking the same thing: decent-paying work, virtually unobtainable in their homelands with rising populations and limited industrialisation.

It remains sadly true that the elite of British Columbia

Members of the Russian Doukhobor sect—believers in communal life and a religion in which the individual, not the church, is paramount—settled in southeastern B.C. in 1908. About 6,000 people started a rural community under their leader Peter Verigin, but it was soon split by dissent and fanaticism. Individuals bought their own, private homes. The terrorist Sons of Freedom group burned schools to protest provincial compulsory education. The Depression and terrorism combined to destroy the community and their land was taken over by the province. There was another flare-up of violence and nude parades from 1950 to 1960, but now Doukhobors—about 15,000—concentrate on keeping their cultural heritage alive.

and their working-class allies did their best to keep Asians out of the country, and to make their lives miserable if they got in. A series of laws and administrative devices were aimed at non-white immigrants. Egged on by newspapers, pressure groups and workers worried about cheap labour, the legislature introduced head taxes, quotas, literacy tests and restricted job opportunities. Most, but not all, of these crudely-disguised tricks were rejected by Ottawa or the courts.

Sikhs like these—350 of them—sailed to Vancouver in July 1914 aboard the Komogata Maru, *a freighter chartered by a wealthy businessman. But they were forbidden to land and, after skirmishes with officials, the rusty old cruiser* HMCS Rainbow *was called in to stand guard. Eventually the Sikhs sailed home. The Sikhs' trip was undoubtedly an attempt to test Canadian immigration laws. But who was behind it? The Sikhs—or German agents seeking to stir up trouble in India and in North America?*

When politics failed, there was always violence. Vancouver had its first race riot on February 24, 1887, when it was less than a year old. A mob wrecked a camp in False Creek full of Chinese labourers just laid off by the CPR. Then on September 7, 1907 another mob listened to speeches at an Asiatic Exclusion League meeting and stormed off to wreck Chinatown. The rioters met little resistance. They moved to Little Tokyo but found the Japanese, proud of their Imperial Navy's trouncing of Russia in the 1905 war, less submissive. Fighting broke out until a truce was called. The Chinese had the last laugh, however. Two days after the attack there was a general strike of all Chinese workers, and many matrons had todo thei own washing. By the 1920s the racists had won. Immigration of non-whites was just a trickle and stayed that way for 30 years.

When war came in August, 1914 there were only two small sloops and the old-fashioned cruiser *HMCS Rainbow* to defend the Pacific coast. Out in the Pacific, it was believed, lurked a German cruiser squadron ready to sink ships and attack Vancouver. As a quick fix the province bought two submarines, built for the Chilean navy, from a Seattle shipyard—and then handed them over to the Royal Canadian Navy. Coastal defence guns were hastily installed at Point Grey to protect Burrard inlet and at

Just before the war ended—on October 28, 1918—the CPR's Princess Sophia *ran up on a reef just out of Skagway on a trip to Vancouver. For three days, the 346 passengers and crew waited for rescue but the weather was too bad. The* Sophia *slipped off the reef and went down with everyone on board. In peacetime, the news would have filled the newspapers and been the subject of talk for days. But Allied troops were close to victory and the Spanish flu epidemic was raging (522 cases were reported in Vancouver on October 27) and so the* Sophia *was soon forgotten.*

Stanley Park to protect the harbour. A detachment of 300 men was sent to Prince Rupert to protect the new harbour there. But no German raiders came and after a few months it was obvious that the Pacific coast would not see any action.

Most of the immigrants who had come to the province in the last 30 years or so came from Britain. In those days patriotism was a simpler affair and thousands of British Columbians were soon on their way to Britain to train for the trenches and die by their thousands in France. Back in Vancouver, the men who stayed and thousands of women started work in shipyards, machine shops and munition factories. The sinking of the liner *Lusitania* by a German submarine off the Irish coast on May 24, 1915 led to anti-German riots in Victoria. Hotels and shops with German names or believed to be owned by Germans were attacked.

Women soldiers parade in Hastings Park, Vancouver, 1915. Women have often gone to war—usually as camp followers and nurses. In the First World War women enlisted in the armed services for the first time and did many of the jobs formerly done by men.

When war came again in 1940, the inlet and the harbour were protected by two groups of six-inch naval guns at Point Grey and Stanley Park. Emplacements with searchlights and listening

After being seized in December 1941 by the Canadian Navy, these Japanese fishboats are moored near Steveston to await reconditioning before being sold. The high cost of reconditioning—which was often done unnecessarily—and other costs meant that their owners recovered pitifully small sums for their boats.

posts were built, but the guns never fired. In 1942, an American freighter was torpedoed off Vancouver Island and the naval station at Estevan Point was shelled by a Japanese submarine, but the great naval and land battles of the Pacific war were being fought thousands of miles away.

In Vancouver and Victoria the shipyards worked to capacity and they hired more than 30,000 people to build freighters and small naval ships. The race to join the armed forces was less eager than in 1914, but large numbers of men were soon in Europe. Some died at Dieppe or in their bombers over Germany, but most had to wait until 1944 before they met the Germans. Back home, women built ships and airplanes and made electrical equipment for guns, ships and planes.

Fifty years of discrimination against Japanese immigrants and their Canadian-born children came to a head in the winter of 1941-42. Soon after the Japanese attacked Pearl Harbour in December 1941, Japanese fishermen

1942: Japanese Canadians start on the journey away from their homes on the coast toward internment camps in the Interior of B.C. or to the Prairies. Many would not come back, preferring to move to Ontario or to return to Japan.

were rounded up and their boats were seized. Then—early in 1942—20,881 Japanese Canadians were expelled from their homes on the coast. After being registered in the Pacific National Exhibition sheds, they were shipped to hastily-built camps in the interior or to sugarbeet farms on the prairies. The property they left behind was sold at ridiculously low prices. Soon after the war ended, it became obvious that the expulsion was generated by locally-fomented racism. National security was not at risk.

Between the two wars was the Great Depression. The conventional story of the Depression of the 1930s goes like this: after a time of extravagance and pleasure-seeking, booze, short skirts and stockings rolled above the knee, the economy collapsed and hard times were had by all.

The reality, particularly in B.C., is somewhat different. The twenties were not only the time of the flapper. They were also the time of soup kitchens in the cities and poverty in the Interior. Forestry and mining were prospering, but the fishing industry still felt the effects of the Hells' Gate slide of 1913 when dynamiting by contractors building the Canadian Northern Railway sent tons of rock into the Fraser River and well-nigh destroyed the sockeye salmon run. There was no plan to absorb the thousands of discharged servicemen seeking jobs and wartime factories stayed silent.

For the man without a job, a home, or a family, there was only the hard bench and the gnawing awareness that tomorrow would be no better, perhaps even worse.

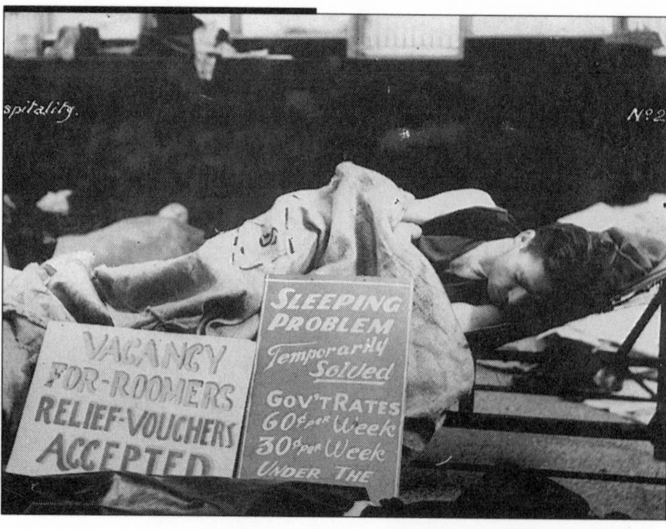

On October 29, 1929, the stock exchange crash reverberated through North America and Europe. Orders were cancelled, loans called, factories shut and workers sent home. Prime Minister Mackenzie King said: "Business was never better," but almost everyone except the politicians and a few shortsighted businessmen knew otherwise—particularly in British Columbia. Two months into the Depression, eight days before Christmas, unemployed men were besieging a Vancouver relief office.

Number gathering was not the science it is today and no-one knows how many lost their jobs and sought relief. Best estimates are that in the City of Vancouver, for example, 8,000 families were on relief and that 40,000 were "just hanging on." About 28 per cent of workers were unemployed. Across Canada, 1,350,000 were on relief.

The depression struck the suburbs of Vancouver differently. In 1930, West Vancouver had only 20 unemployed. Soon, however, there was work for everyone as land was prepared for British Pacific Properties, controlled by the Guinness family. The Guinesses told the municipality that they wanted to buy 4,000 acres of land to build an exclusive residential suburb with a bridge across the inlet at First Narrows. Agreement about access for the bridge through Stanley Park took time and the Lions Gate Bridge was not built until 1938, at a cost of six million dollars. The bridge allows 1,550 feet of channel for shipping. Tolls were charged until 1963 when the provincial government bought the bridge.

Another conventional image is that a widespread blanket of gloom stretched over the land. The truth is that there were pockets, small indeed, of comfort and happiness. The misery of British Columbia was nothing compared to that of the Atlantic provinces. And if the husband kept his job, life was comfortable indeed, for prices were low (a hamburger 10 cents; a movie 50 cents), maids would work for almost nothing and rents were cheap.

But for the jobless, the old and poor, life was hard indeed. There were none of the systems of today that bring not only money but also security to people hit by economic distress. There was no unemployment insurance, no social security system underwritten by Ottawa and run by the provinces. Relief came from the municipalities, and they did not have the resources to cope with poverty on this massive level. The municipality of West Vancouver was barely affected, but the other municipalities around Vancouver went bankrupt, despite help from the provincial and federal governments, and were taken over by commissioners.

All the attention was focussed on the single males who protested, rioted, were put in relief and forestry camps and demanded money. Forgotten were the old, particularly old Chinese people, and single women living away from their families.

Most politicians did virtually nothing, for they believed that the capitalist system, which had survived downturns

Strikes and violence in B.C.
1850: Fort Rupert coal miners.
Turn of the century: Nanaimo coal miners, Fraser fishermen, Kootenay miners, CPR workers.
1910: Railway workers, coal miners.
B.C. Federation of Labour was formed in 1910; Wobblies very active in this period.
1911: GTP workers at Prince Rupert, Crow's Nest coal miners.
1913: Nanaimo coal miners
1917: Crow's Nest miners.
1918: Vancouver longshoremen, shipyard workers, transit workers, Vancouver General Strike.
1919: Vancouver workers support Winnipeg General Strike.
1929-39: Depression.
1952: B.C. Woodworkers.
1983: Solidarity vs Bill Bennett.

in the past, would soon rebound. Spending money on relief and work projects was not only unnecesssary—it was foolish. Balanced budgets were the key to economic growth. Labour unions had no place for unemployed members and so it was natural for the unemployed to listen to new leaders and to organisations such as the Workers Unity League, mostly led by Communists.

British Columbia's climate lured the jobless and homeless from across the country and young single men, riding the freight cars to the coast, added to the numbers demanding food, money and a place to sleep. Municipal and provincial politicians demanded help from Ottawa and, after long delays and pompous speeches from Prime Minister R.B. Bennett, some came. Then came the construction of relief and forestry camps in the Interior to get the unemployed out of Vancouver. With virtually no pay, poor food and no women, the camps were breeding grounds for riots, if not revolt, and many of the men flocked back to Vancouver.

Leaders of the unemployed organised protests to get public attention and to frighten the already terrified politicians. There was a march of 15,000 people through Vancouver in March 1932. On April 23, 1935, about

Depression riots in Vancouver.

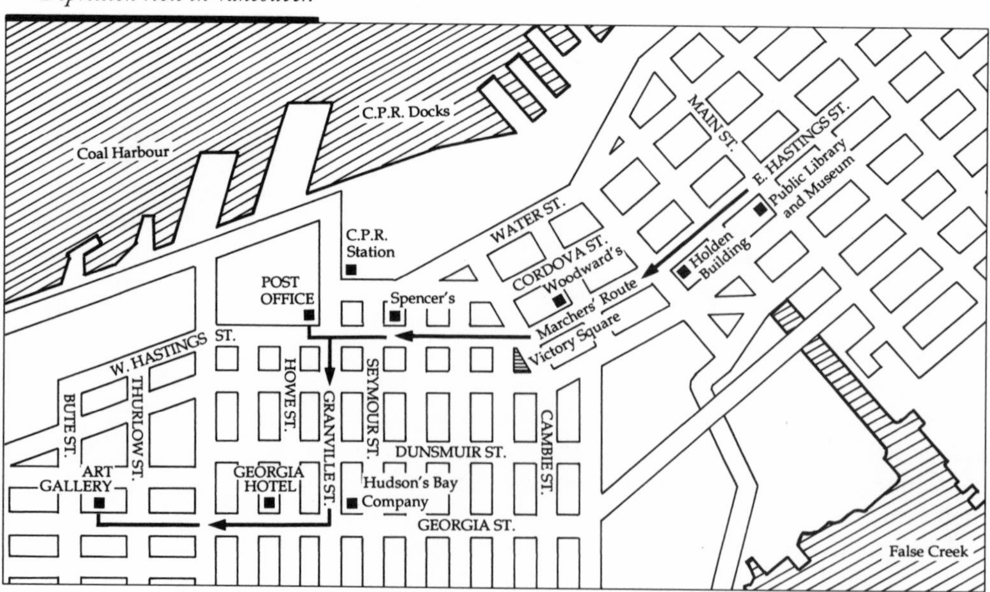

1,400 people occupied the Hudson's Bay store at Georgia and Granville. When they were forced out, the men marched to Victory Square and Mayor Gerry McGeer read the Riot Act.

On May 16, the men occupied the City Library at Hastings and Main and then decided to ride the trains to Ottawa; but when they reached Regina their camp was surrounded by troops and police.

Tear gas ends month-long occupation of the Vancouver Post Office by jobless men, June 1938.

The best-planned and biggest act of defiance came on May 20, 1938, when 700 men evaded the police and slipped into the Post Office at Granville and Hastings. 300 took over the Hotel Georgia and 200 quietly moved into the Art Gallery on Georgia. Those in the Hotel Georgia left after being paid money by city aldermen, but many of those in the Post Office and Art Gallery stayed until the early morning of Sunday, June 20, when they were ejected by the RCMP with tear gas.

Nothing really changed for a year, and then the war came. Strangely, money was found to feed and house the men—and give them work to do.

Depression statistics:
Spring 1930: 7,000 people on relief in Vancouver
February 1932: 67,000 jobless in Vancouver out of a total population of 694,000; in February 1933, 100,000 were out of work.
1932: 8,000 of Burnaby's total population of 25,000 were out of work.
March 1933: 1,360,000 Canadians were on relief.
There was no accurate system measuring unemployment, the workforce, or welfare assistance. There was no unemployment insurance. Relief was administered by provincial, municipal, religious and private institutions and was largely based on the thesis that unemployment and povety were self-inflicted and sinful.

A Three-Bedroom House in Revelstoke

April 24, 1935

"You know—until now I always felt sorry for those poor guys who used to come through here, clinging to the boxcars on their way to the coast."

Ulf Gustafson is, as usual, giving his wife and children his opinions on the topics of the day at suppertime. He manages a drug store for his wife's father and does very well, thank you, in these days when about a quarter of the workers in British Columbia haven't got jobs.

He carries on munching his veal steak, potatoes and cabbage. His wife, Rosa, is always telling their children not to talk while they are eating, but Ulf is different. He is a man and the breadwinner—even if the store does belong to her father.

"After all, it just made sense to come here. The Maritimes were never what you'd call hotbeds of prosperity, even when times were better. Ontario used to have all those factory jobs that went down the spout, once no-one wanted to buy cars, or railway locomotives, or whatever. And it gets bloody cold there, too. The Prairies—don't you forget, kids, that was where I grew up—well, they were doing fine but scratching every ounce of wheat out of the land and putting little back. Wheat miners, not farmers, they were. Once the drought and winds came it was a dustbowl like in those movies your mother sees—ones about sheiks and slaves and arabs. Cold, too."

Edmonton Grads Once More Canadian Basket Champs

PAGE SQUAD TAKES THIRD GAME 44-31

Twelfth Dominion Crown for Prairie Girl Quintet

WINDSOR Canadian basketball crown

Rosa smiles. He's a hardnosed man, she knows, giving little away in business and showing little affection to her or the children. Perhaps that's the way it has to be these days. But he can still tease her and the children every now and then. She's happy that he's a good provider and a reliable, if unsympathetic, father. Why, the other day he was even talking—in his joking way, of course—about adding to their family. Might get a real man this time, he said. Better than that book-reading, namby-pamby son of yours.

Another baby would be nice, she thought. Thank God she wasn't terrified of getting pregnant, like some of her friends whose husbands had been laid off and only worked every now and then for a couple of bucks or some food.

Her daughter Joan interrupts," But the poor lads didn't look very happy when they came through. It's not exactly warm, you know, on most days. There's always a cold wind. But I suppose it was worth it when they got to Vancouver."

"Jimmy told me some of them were sunbathing on the beach at some place called English Bay," says Andrew, eight, in between mouthfuls of veal. He starts to take some more potatoes but stops when he remembers that his favourite—steamed pudding with jam—is for dessert.

"Don't be stupid," says Joan, who is thirteen. "The poor men have nothing else to do. Why shouldn't they enjoy themselves a little? I read in a book once that everyone's entitled to their seat in the sun."

"Anyway," says Ulf, "I think that Mayor McGeer in Vancouver has the right idea. He read the Riot Act in Victory Square yesterday after they had stormed through the Hudson's Bay, wrecked the place and then gallivanted through the streets. Thank God the cops nabbed and charged 19 of 'em. I can't understand all those people cheering them and giving them coffee and doughnuts. Never should have been allowed to leave those camps they put them in after they got to Vancouver. Then they let them get back into the city and see what you've got—it's a revolution. At least they had food and a roof over their heads when they were in the camps, and everyone knew what they were up to.

"Tony—he sits next to me in class—says the camps are awful, Dad." Andrew is talking. He doesn't like to contradict his father; sometimes his father's anger mounts up and Andrew has to bear the brunt of it with a whipping. But now he sees his mother smiling at him.

"Dad—Tony says they get awful food and have nothing to do, nowhere to go. The army's running some of the camps like there was a war on."

"What's wrong with that?—and where are you going, Joan, before you've got permission to leave the table?"

"Mother said this afternoon that I can go to the Roxy with Doreen and her sister."

"And did your mother take the trouble to find out what picture you're seeing? I don't want you gawping at some love-sick trash that will give you silly ideas at your age."

Rosa butts in before there are tears at the dinner table.

"It's *The Good Fairy,* with Margaret

Sullavan and Herbert Marshall and if they're in it, I'm certain there will be nothing that a girl of 13 can't see."

But Ulf wants to get back to the serious business.

"I thought that Mayor McGeer's speech on the radio made some sense. He's saying that it's stupid to put people in jail for wanting jobs when there are $20,000,000 worth of public works projects waiting to be done in Vancouver alone. Ottawa should find some money to help these men. But not one cent is going to leave city coffers to help them, he says."

Ulf stops for breath while his wife clears the plates away.

"Come to think of it, there are a lot of things like roads and lights that need fixing around here. But first they should get all those unemployed, and the rabble-rousers who tell them what to do, back in the camps so that everyone can find some time to let things settle down."

Joan comes down from her room with her new dress on.

"And how much was that?" her father asks.

"A dollar at Woodward's," says her mother. "Mrs. Stimpson brought it back for me when she went on that trip to Vancouver. By the way, do you know she's trying to get her husband to take her to the Silver Jubilee in London? She says Canadian National is offering a round trip for $200. I'd love to go."

"And what would happen to those stupid families you're always on about? The ones who can't live on the relief money and won't

The Daily World

THE LARGEST MORNING PAPER CIRCULATION IN WESTERN CANADA

CIRCULATION YESTERDAY 18,414 VANCOUVER, B.C., THURSDAY, APRIL 25, 1935

ACE MOVE FOR CAMP STRIKERS

Mayor Calls Conference Of Labor Men, Strikers To End Jobless Crisis

McGeer Hails Plan as First Step Toward Settlement

VANCOUVER, APRIL 25—

BIG STRIKE LOOMS

Will Urge Men to Return to Camps Pending Result of Probe

work? The Williamses, for example. They scrounge from you and you buy them food—out of the money that I work hard everyday to earn."

"It doesn't cost much and you and the children don't suffer. I see to that," Rosa replies. "I buy them tripe, and beef shanks and stew for seven cents a pound. Sometimes for a treat I get them hamburger—it's the same price! And I try to buy large quantities. Like a four-pound jar of marmalade—it's about 31 cents. Or three pounds of coffee for 70 cents. And as a change, I buy Point Grey herrings. Only 15 cents for three pounds! Surely you don't mind my doing that? They are still our friends even if they are ashamed to come around these days. Can't you imagine what it's like to have nothing now—and nothing to look forward to? Let alone worrying all night about how you're going to feed your four kids and keep clothes on their backs and see they're warm?"

Her husband grunts.

"Fine thing. We can't give them money because she's stupid enough to let him grab it all to buy cheap booze. And you give them clothes and furniture! Last month you gave them that old washstand."

But he doesn't complain too much. In these times, perhaps a helping hand might be a good idea. He'd like to think that the families Rosa helped were shiftless and undeserving. But it made her happy and if she let him have a beer on the way home from the store, well, it was worth it.

Joan's friends have come to pick her up. They whisper and giggle together in the hall, and then leave. Andrew and his parents eat their dessert in silence, then he goes to his room to do his homework.

"Now they're gone, Ulf. Have you read in the paper about that Mrs. Rattenbury? Her poor husband—you know the one—he built the Legislature Buildings and the Empress in Victoria. Francis, that's his name. He's been stabbed over in England and she and her boyfriend the gardener have been charged. What a case!"

Her husband doesn't much care about idle gossip. He goes to his chair and starts to read the paper. There's a list of the clashes between the rioters and the police, speeches by outraged politicians and the names of the men who have been charged.

"Serves 'em right. All of them!"

OPPENHEIMER BROS.

COMMISSION MERCHANTS,
IMPORTERS AND WHOLESALE DEALERS
IN

GROCERIES
And Provisions!

WHARF STREET, VICTORIA, B.C.

HAVING ESTABLISHED BUSINESS IN THE ABOVE LINES AND BY
RECENT IMPORTATIONS
FROM
EUROP'AN & EAST'RN MARK'TS
We are prepared to Fill orders to the trade
IN THE FOLLOWING GOODS:

TEAS, COFFEES, SUGARS, TOBACCOS

HAM, BACON, LARD, CODFISH, MACKEREL, CANDLES, RICE, SYRUP, CHEESE, DRIED FRUITS, CANNED GOODS, VINEGAR, BAKING POWDER, SOAP, COAL OIL, COCOA, PEARL BARLEY, BEANS, BROOMS, PAPER BAGS, WRAPPING PAPER, AND ALL OTHER GOODS
IN THE GROCERY AND PROVISION LINE

SPECIAL ATTENTION!

Is called to the undernoted Goods, on which the most Liberal Inducements will be offered to the Trade, as we are

Sole Agents for British Columbia.

GOOD AS GOLD BAKING POWDER, THE BEST AND THE CHEAPEST;
BEACON LIGHT COAL OIL; WATER WHITE AND PURE;
ARTIC SUGAR CURED HAM,
TURKISH PATROL CIGARETTES; BEING THE LARGEST SIZE AND BEST TABACCO

☛ *Our Goods are Guaranteed of the Highest Standard in Quality and are offered at the* Lowest Market Rates.

Victoria's old Legislative Building—the Birdcages.

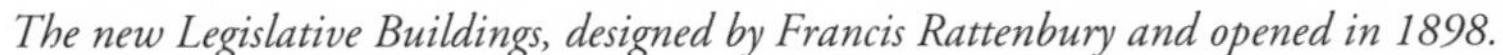

The new Legislative Buildings, designed by Francis Rattenbury and opened in 1898.

AT LAST, THE GOOD LIFE 1950 to 1991

W.A.C. Snatches Power From Corrupt Coalition

Dams and Universities Send B.C. into Modern Age

Socred Dream Turns Sour

Environment and Native Rights Demand Action

AROUND THE WORLD
KOREA — 1950 Canada sends troops, aircraft and ships to join the Korean War
SOUTH VIETNAM — 1975 Saigon surrenders to Communists from the north
SOVIET UNION — 1985 Gorbachev starts perestroika and glasnost leading to end of Soviet empire.

*POPULATION — 1981	
Native People	73,670 (2.7%)
British	1,505,467 (55.5%)
Other Europeans	874,269 (32.3%)
Asian	204,856 (7.5%)
Other	55,353 (2%)
Total	2,713,615

*ETHNIC ORIGIN

Until now this history of British Columbia has focussed on events. Strong personalities—men like Sir James Douglas and Cornelius Van Horne—have played their roles but events have outshone the players. But after the second world war, events became less significant and personalities became more so. The growth of television and other mass media helped the voter make personality the dominant feature of public life. Ironically, this resulted in an increasing disillusion with politicians and the political process—and a corresponding rise in single-issue groups and splinter parties.

One man, William Andrew Cecil Bennett, ruled public life in British Columbia from 1952 to 1972. And his influence lasted for another 19 years until it ended, whimpering, in the 1991 Social Credit election campaign.

Like many other political leaders, Bennett persevered through years of political failure

W.A.C. Bennett (centre, second row from top) at school in New Brunswick.

Social Credit's ideology, the child of Major Clifford Douglas, was widely debated in England just after the first world war and it spread to Canada before the Depression. In its simplest form, Social Credit tried to cure the imbalance between production and consumption. Douglas came to Canada and spoke to a Kiwanis meeting and to the Provincial Legislature in 1934. But the candidates who ran for the Social Credit league did poorly over the next years. Then the decay of the Liberal-Conservative coalition offered a chance for an alternative party. W.A.C. Bennett resigned from the Conservatives, became an independent MLA, and joined Social Credit in 1951. There was a tussle with the Albertan Social Crediters—they claimed to hold the right to Social Credit, and saw B.C. as a fiefdom for control. But Bennett dealt with them and brought his own brand of Social Credit—and political success—to B.C.

and scorn. He was born in New Brunswick in 1901, and came to Kelowna as a young married man with children in 1930. He was a Conservative, and he believed in the values of hard work and thrift and in the word of the *Bible.* For celebrations he preferred Ovaltine and for reading material he chose long columns of figures.

Bennett ruled by the force of his personality. He was a brilliant salesman and could create instant visions to dazzle his colleagues and the voters. Since he had no real political ideology, he could switch easily from policy to policy without a tremor. Bennett had switched from the federal to the provincial Conservatives twice before he joined the British Columbia Social Credit party, then an offshoot of the Alberta party run by Premier Ernest Manning, just before the election of June 12, 1952.

The years since the war were prosperous times for British Columbia as the damage caused by the war in Europe was repaired and the hungry and homeless were fed and housed. But there were no riches in the political purse. The Liberal-Conservative coalition, peopled by mediocrities united only by an almost paranoid fear of the CCF, squabbled and offered little leadership or example. And when they introduced, just before the 1952 election, a complicated multiple-choice voting system to make certain that the socialists did not slip into power by dividing the free enterprise vote, they delivered their own death blow. The new system took the anti-socialist vote and applied it to make the Socreds—not the Liberals or Conservatives—the winners. The upstarts got 19 seats to the CCF's 18, in a 48-seat house.

Bennett's political luck, which had spurned him for 20 years, now lodged firmly on his shoulder. He took power on August 1, 1952, at a time of powerful growth. Investment was pouring into the province for pipelines, factories, refineries, lumber and pulp mills. Pay packets were full. Government revenues increased, and there was plenty of money to build highways, bridges and create even more jobs.

Bennett quickly tidied up the hospital insurance scheme that had been bungled by the coalition, got his allies Robert Bonner and Einar Gunderson into the House—they had not even run in the election—and brought in a "pay-as-you-go" budget. Then he engineered a defeat in the House so that he could call an election and get a working majority. This he did on June 12, 1953, getting 28 seats to the CCF's 14. When the cumbersome counting process was over the Socreds' popular vote was close to 46 per cent.

Bennett now saw a clear road ahead and began to show investors, businessmen and the public that he could run an exciting government, pleasing to almost everyone in the province. A massive roads and highways program, presided over by the eccentric highways minister, Phil Gaglardi, pushed blacktop through the province. The Pacific Great Eastern railway was extended north, bridges, tunnels and schools were built. Bennett, ever the magician with figures, designed an ingenious financial scheme which, in effect, transferred parts of the provincal debt to corporations running schools, bridges and roads. He then claimed to have lifted the burden of debt from the province.

Premier Bennett never rejected a chance to celebrate. Here he enjoys himelf as the northern extension of the PGE is opened at Prince George.

From the middle 1950s, Premier Bennett soared from success to success in the eyes of the public. Not even a bribery scandal caused by the conduct of Forestry Minister Robert Sommers left any stain on Bennett. In the 1956 election, under a simple majority system, he got 46 per cent of the vote. Within two years, however, Bennett's

Bennett's plans transform the interior of B.C. The Pacific Great Eastern (now B.C. Rail) connects the towns and villages—and the mills, gas wells and factories—of the north with the Lower Mainland. Hydro dams are built on the Columbia and Peace Rivers to provide the power for industrial growth.

Columbia dams: Duncan, built in 1967, is 130 feet high with a 28-mile long reservoir; Keenleyside, built in 1968, is 170 feet high with a 145-mile long reservoir. Mica, built in 1973, is 800 feet high with a 16-mile long reservoir.

Peace dams: Bennett, built in 1967, is 600 feet high with a 410,000 acre reservoir; Peace Canyon, built in 1980, is 70 feet high with a 13-mile long reservoir.

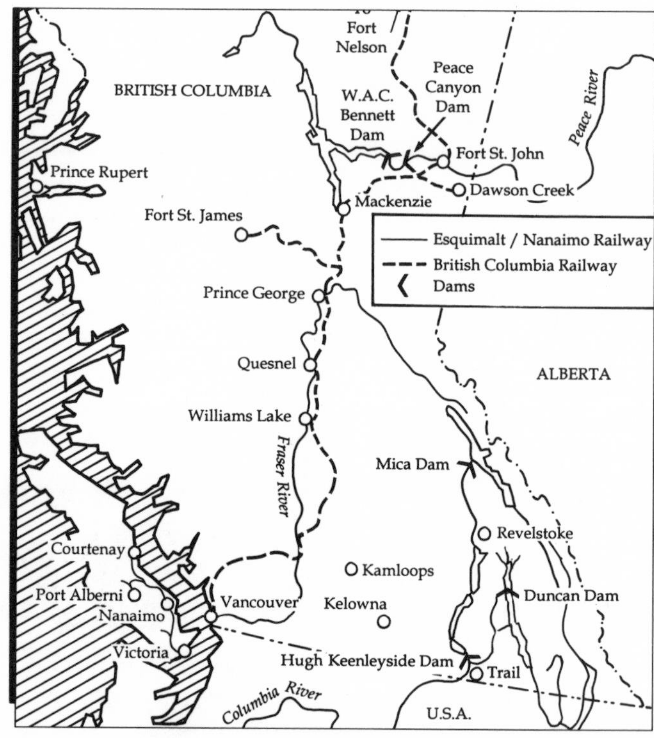

blue skies were clouding over. Strikes, shutdowns and protests cast doubts on the Bennett magic. And so, on February 12, 1957, the Socreds unveiled a development plan that would dwarf all others. A Swedish industrialist, Axel Wenner Gren, with a murky reputation during the war and a very bad track record in fulfilling promises, had agreed to develop the Peace River Trench stretching for hundreds of miles in the northern Interior. A monorail would connect pulp mills, towns, power stations, colleges and all the apparatus of a modern industrial state. In return, Wenner Gren got a monopoly in development in the area, about one-tenth of the province.

But Wenner Gren's plans stayed on the drawing table and Bennett looked for new ways to keep the adrenalin flowing in the province. Ottawa had been arguing with the U.S. for years about how to develop the power locked up in the Columbia River. Now Bennett, never one to let slip a chance of embarrassing Ottawa, trumpeted his vision of

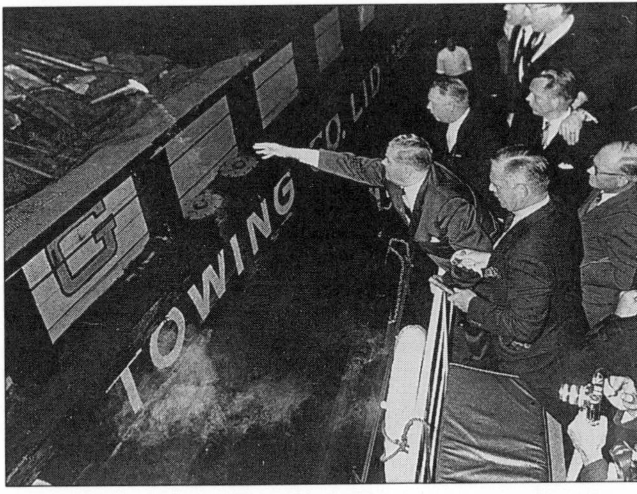

Premier Bennett at his bond-burning ceremony.

Peace River power. Giant dams and an immense artificial lake would provide cheap power to the Lower Mainland and transform northern B.C.

After some fast financial footwork, Bennett declared that British Columbia was debt-free, and on August 2, 1959, in a ceremony suited more to the Shriners' circus than to politics, he shot a flaming arrow into a raft carrying the government's cancelled bonds. (The indirect debt, guaranteed by the government, was still there.) And when the unions shut down the private ferry service between Vancouver Island and the Mainland, the premier—in a master stroke—decided that the government would take over the service.

After the 1960 election, in which the Social Credit vote

In July 1958 a strike stopped ferry service between the Mainland and Vancouver Island. Premier Bennett asked Ottawa to intervene. He also talked with the union and employers, without success. The province, using the Civil Defence Act, started operating the ferries. The strikers went back to work but Bennett had learned enough about ferries to plan his next move. He offered to provide the docks and approach-roads if the ferry companies would improve service. The companies refused. Then, in 1959, the government leased the contracts for two ferries, the Queen of Sidney and the Queen of Tsawwassen, and built docks at Swartz Bay and Tsawwassen for the start of service on June 15, 1960. Bennett bought out Black Ball for $6,800,000 in October 1961 and the CPR soon closed down its ferry service, leaving the B.C. Ferry Corporation running the routes to Victoria, Nanaimo and the Sunshine Coast. Today it has 40 ships—such as the Queen of Vancouver *(left)—on 24 routes, and a staff of 3,000.*

U.S. President Lyndon Johnson, Prime Minister Lester Pearson and Premier Bennett on their way to the Peace Arch to celebrate the Columbia Power Agreement on September 16, 1964. Johnson gives Bennett a cheque for $273,291,661.25—for downstream benefits and flood control.

went down to 39 per cent and the CCF's rose to 33 per cent, the premier turned his attention to the problems of Peace and Columbia power. In the next three years the hardware merchant from Kelowna outplayed Prime Minister John Diefenbaker and Justice Minister Davie Fulton, the ranking B.C. Tory. They sadly mishandled the three-way Columbia power negotiations with the United States and Victoria. Bennett got the terms he wanted. His critics claimed that these were the terms the Americans wanted, too. When the privately-owned B.C. Electric Railway Company balked at joining the premier's Peace River plan, he took over the company and then merged it with the B.C. Power Commission. In the next three years Bennett happily watched the work on the Peace River dam and Columbia dams. Parties, ceremonies, more bond burning—these were the days for Bennett to enjoy—and in the September 1966 election he reached his highest popular vote so far—close to 46 per cent.

But the boom was levelling off and the Socreds' well-paid helpers were getting a little greedy and tarnishing the image of probity. Highways Minister Gaglardi, for example, was accused of helping his sons and friends to profit from government contracts and inside information. Gaglardi resigned, but had done little wrong in Bennett's eyes. For the 1969 election, the usual kind of election tidbits were offered to voters. Money was plentiful, and few parts

Premier W.A.C. Bennett shows off his skills as the builder of modern B.C.

In 1963, Bennett asked Dr. Gordon Shrum to build another University to serve the Fraser Valley. In 1964, the trees on Burnaby Mountain are cut and roads are cut through the bush. In August 1965, Simon Fraser University, designed by Arthur Erickson and Geoffrey Massey, was ready for students.

of the province could claim they had been forgotten. The Socreds got their highest ever popular vote—close to 47 per cent.

But now the once proud Bennett caravan was slowing down. The great achievements which transformed the face of the province—huge dams, miles of blacktop including new arterial highways and bridges, a first-rate ferry system, B.C. Hydro, new universities—were all in place. But the foundation was rotten. Bennett's bravado and political brilliance had faded. Many of his ministers were incompetent clowns who sought confrontation with teachers, doctors, the poor and the unions. Bennett's total control over the Legislature with no Question Period, no real Hansard and no desire to share power with the MLAs, even of his own party, now seemed to be petty and malign instead of bold and purposeful. The real costs of the two-rivers policy, with its massive spending

NDP's Dave Barrett celebrated victory over the tired Socreds in 1972; he arrived at Parliament in a beat-up Volvo. He broke the hold of right-of-centre parties in B.C.—but not for long.

ACHIEVEMENTS:

W.A.C. Bennett
(1952-1972)
Massive highway construction
Massey Tunnel
Port Mann Bridge
Simon Fraser Univerity
University of Victoria
Community Colleges
PGE extensions to N. Interior
B.C. Ferry Corporation
Columbia and Peace R. dams

Dave Barrett
(1972-1975)
Agricultural Land Reserves
Insurance Corp. of B.C.
Question Period and Hansard
Community Resources Board
Human Rights Program
B.C. Development Corp.

Bill Bennett
(1975-1986)
B.C. Coal
B.C. Place
Expo 86
Skytrain
Coquihalla Highway
B.C. Resources Investment Corp.

Bill Vander Zalm
(1986-1991)
Privatisation of:
B.C. Hydro's gas division
B.C. Hydro's railway
Highway maintenance

and agreements with the Americans, were exposed and the premier's crude attacks on Ottawa were disturbing even the government's friends.

On August 30, 1972, after a weak election campaign against a bouncy new NDP leader, Dave Barrett, Bennett's Social Credit party was defeated. Their share of the popular vote sank from 47 to 31 per cent and their seats from 38 to 10. The NDP seized 38 seats with 40 per cent of the vote. When W.A.C. Bennett left office on September 13, 1972, he was driven away by a chauffeur in a Cadillac. When Dave Barrett took over, he arrived at Government House in a slightly-soiled Volvo. The public was ready for change.

It would be nice to report that British Columbia's left-of-centre politicians, who had been fighting to gain power for more than 40 years, seized their chances when they took over. But only a loyal NDP member would claim success. The Bennett regime had created the infrastructure for a highly-industrialised province, and the bigger industries—particularly forestry and mining—had benefited from the improvements in transport and power supply. In 20 years of Socred rule, electrical power generation increased sixfold. The construction industry had grown fat as roads, railways, plants and docks (the Roberts Bank coal port, for example) were built. The trend to bigger firms, integrated both locally and internationally, continued. New universities and colleges sprouted throughout the province. In short, material prosperity was at hand.

Now the NDP, led by a Jewish, Roman Catholic-educated social worker, very sensible of the diversity of the province and of the need for reform, had its chance. Now it could use the power of the state to improve the quality of life in the province as Bennett and his businessmen friends had improved its quantity. And in many areas that happened. The delivery and generosity of social welfare programs were improved immensely when an imaginative system of 23 Community Resource Boards was set up. An urban transit system, years overdue, began to give transit service to the suburbs and neighbouring municipalities. Provincial car insurance and land reserve legislation to curb urban sprawl and protect farmland were introduced in 1973. Farmers got an income assurance plan, and provincial government workers got the right to strike. Taxes were increased for mining companies in 1974, and a number of crown corporations—designed to handle failing forest companies and develop other industries—were formed.

New look for politicians: Just before his defeat at the polls in 1975, Premier Barrett meets the new member of the Social Credit party—former Liberal Bill Vander Zalm.

As if to make up for the years out of power, Barrett made Bennett's race to change the province seem like a dawdle. The legislation enabling these and other changes was pushed swiftly through the House. In the first year of his rule, Barrett introduced 300 important bills into the Legislature, compared with an average of 40 in Bennett's days. But the chief problem was this: the NDP tried to bring about a sophisticated, left-of-centre, Scandinavian-style state with the antiquated bureaucractic and parliamentary system bequeathed it by Bennett. There was no adequate committee structure, and caucus meetings were just friendly get-togethers. Instead of Cabinet being the place where government priorities were discussed and decided, it was an arena in which some of the robber barons of Cabinet diverted parliamentary and financial resources to their own pet projects.

Premier Bennett had been the mainspring of most of his government's operations and, through his financial expertise and conspiratorial techniques, could both direct operations and sense when anything was off course. His staffing needs were small. Premier Barrett, however, was the leader of a Cabinet with members who quickly recognised that a good bureaucracy was the foundation of success in winning over Cabinet. Those members who made the best presentations got the resources. This distorted the government's priorities and, unfortunately, meant that good budgeting was almost impossible to achieve—and this in a time of limited economic growth.

Barrett, who should have had the staff—and the ability—to control the robber barons and their plans, had neither until the arrival of Marc Eliesen from the NDP in Ottawa. By then it was probably too late. (Twenty years later, Eliesen again was called west—this time to head B.C. Hydro.)

The perception that Barrett could not control his ministers was heightened by the inability of the NDP to explain and justify their policies. Convinced of their own abilities and a little heady with success, the Cabinet and Barrett's advisors did not seem to realise that—to many businessmen and most of the folk in the Interior—they were still the "Red Horde". Superb public relations were essential to calm their fears. Instead there was insensivity and a sense of "we are the masters now."

This meant that after three years, when most governments are usually getting into their stride, the NDP was starting to stumble. For some reason, Barrett decided to call an election for December 11, 1975, instead of using the next months to prepare a campaign. His loyal supporters did not desert him and the NDP held on to its popular vote of 39 per cent. But the Socreds, revived under W.A.C. Bennett's son Bill, were helped by Liberal and Conservative voters. They got 49 per cent—a return to the figures of W.A.C.

Carrying on: Hardware merchant W.A.C. Bennett shows young sons Bill (left) and Russell how to carry on the family business. And soon after he was defeated in 1972, Bennett started to reorganise the party so that son Bill could carry on the business of the premier's office.

Dave Barrett lost his seat as well as the Premier's office, but the whole province was the loser, for Barrett was a witty, compassionate, mercurial man whose rule was refreshingly free of the taint of financial scandal. He deserved more than a little help from his friends.

Powerful fathers always cast shadows over their sons. Throughout Bill Bennett's political life from 1975 to 1986, he seemed to carry the burden of comparison with his father wearily and sought both to confirm his heritage and, at the same time, to reject it. He confirmed it by embarking on grand schemes such as B.C. Coal, Expo and the British Columbia Resources Investment Corporation—as his father did. He rejected it by choosing to lead a team rather than be a one-man show, and to transform the machinery of government—something his father would never have done.

Wherever you travel in B.C. you will find mines—coal or hardrock metal. The major coal-producing areas are the Bullmoose-Quintette region near Fort St. John, and the five mines of the East Kootenays.

Today the dams, bridges, ferries, highways and unversities his father built are powerful memorials to his energy and political skills. But Bill Bennett's B.C. Place is home only to the B.C. Lions, tractor pulls and sales shows. B.C. Coal seems set to become a billion-dollar black hole and Expo 86 is now just another piece of real estate owned by a wily financier from Hong Kong. BCRIC, Bennett's attempt to bring the wonders of people's capitalism to the masses, is just an unpleasant memory. Skytrain, the exciting automated elevated train system, is a technical success but experts are still wondering whether the technology has cost far too much. Unfortunately, nearly all these projects—and the less spectacular but essential legislation—were wrapped in a web of confusion, half-truths and bitter confrontation. The result was that even the successes seem tainted.

Bill Bennett, who was born on April 14, 1932, owed his start in politics to two people—his father and Grace McCarthy, his father's political daughter. After the 1972 defeat, McCarthy, who had been a favourite cabinet minister since December 1966, and another former cabinet minister, Dan Campbell, tramped the province and kept the spirit of Social Credit alive. In Kelowna, Victoria

The Bennett family—W.A.C., wife May, and their sons Bill (left) and Russell—in a festive mood.

and Vancouver, Bennett Senior cajoled friends and political debtors so that his son became his political heir. Three Liberal MLAs—Pat McGeer, Garde Gardom and Alan Williams—and Tory Hugh Curtis left their parties to join the young Bennett. And so did the young Dutch-born mayor of Surrey, a Liberal named Wim Vander Zalm.

These MLAs would be in Bill Bennett's first cabinet in December 1975 which set about correcting NDP errors. Hydro, ferry and auto insurance costs were increased and Vander Zalm, the Human Resources Minister, started to demolish the new social welfare system. Unfortunately, though some of the new Bennett government's moves could be justified, they were accompanied by bullying or sneering statements that undercut their value.

The rest of Bennett's first session did little to show that he could match his father's skills in selling his policies to the voters. True, new legislation, based on a report by UBC's Dr. Peter Pearse, tidied up and modernised the government's relations with the forest industry. A tight rein on public-service wage increases and on expenditures in general brought a surplus in the government's financial accounts. But Transport Minister Jack Davis blotted his copybook by defrauding the government in a banal airline ticket scheme; a redistribution plan made the government look foolish as it denied involvement and then had to back-pedal.

The Social Credit 1979 election campaign was launched by the premier when he laid out the details of his plan to give the public shares in BCRIC, the British Columbia Resources Investment Corporation. Most of the crown

B.C. Place under construction: under the dome there will be room for football, tractor pulls, and trade shows.

corporations created by the NDP were incorporated in the new entity and the people, not the state, were to be the owners. With BCRIC as his banner, Bennett won his second election. The NDP was two percentage points (46 to 48) and five seats (26 to 31) behind.

In Bennett's scheme everyone in B.C. would get five free shares and any Canadian could buy up to 5,000. Soon there were about 10,000,000 free shares in the hands of British Columbians; 80,000,000 extra shares had been bought through banks and dealers—many by people who borrowed to get the cash. BCRIC was listed on the Vancouver Stock Exchange on August 7, 1979, at $6.12, 12 cents above face value. A year later it was selling at about the same price. Then BCRIC president David Helliwell announced his company would buy a controlling interest in Kaiser Resources at $55 a share. Market

Skytrain's driverless, computer-controlled trains now serve Vancouver, Burnaby, New Westminster and Surrey. This Skytrain unit glides past Science World, two witnesses to Premier Bennett's big-project policy.

Coal from the Bullmoose and Quintette mines, south of Dawson Creek, is loaded onto a freighter at Ridley Island, near Prince Rupert.

experts pointed out that the same deal could have been made a little earlier at $44 a share. The media claimed that a number of people had done very well by buying into Kaiser just before the sale. Another scandal. Another enquiry absolving the principles of wrong doing. But the damage had been done. Helliwell quit and by May 1981, BCRIC was selling at $5.50; a year later it sold at $2.95. The government removed restrictions on share ownership and made it just another company. Then it slowly faded away.

In spring 1980, it was time for the premier to announce some big projects. Vancouver would get a sports stadium the equal of any in North America, an international transportation exposition, a trade centre and a rapid-transit system to link them all with the Lower Mainland. As the months passed a series of land deals, grants from Ottawa, bond issues and other financial arrangements was cobbled together to provide the money. The stadium was rushed ahead and built on budget. Bennett proudly opened it in November 1982 when he switched on the fans to blow up the stadium's teflon roof. The rest of the package did not arrive until the end of his reign.

Next it was B.C. Coal's turn. After years of meetings and rumours, Don Phillips—the Minister for Economic Development—announced that B.C. was going to sign an agreement with the Japanese to supply coal from deposits in the northeast. Eight million tons a year for 15 years, it was announced on January 21, 1981, would be dug from the massive open cast pits. Ottawa was going to contribute $100,000,000 worth of work on a coal port at Prince Rupert and on upgrading Canadian National rail links. B.C. would pay for the new railway lines, townsites, highways and power stations. Critics quickly maintained that this infrastructure would cost about $1 billion—and that the price to the Japanese was a give-away. The pits, however, were dug, ports and railways built and families moved into the new towns. Eventually coal was on its way to Japanese smelters. Critics continued to complain about the cost over-runs and the creative accounting. By 1990, the world price of coal had dropped, the Japanese wanted to re-negotiate, and one of the firms running the pits was in financial trouble. Years of argument and mediation have dulled the lustre of B.C. coal. One cynic said that it would have been cheaper to have told the Japanese that if they did the digging themselves they could have the coal for free.

The recession of 1981-82 provided the background for Bennett's fight with labour that would last almost until he decided to resign. In February 1982, he told the province that he was setting limits on government expenditures and

Bill Bennett's restraint budget brings out the crowds of protest. 20,000 people surround the Legislature on July 27, 1983. Bennett has a bodyguard, but no-one is hurt as Solidarity takes over the unofficial political opposition.

on raises for civil servants. They were asking for raises that averaged 27 per cent and, since Bennett offered 6.5, it was obvious that confrontation was near. On April 6, 30,000 civil servants walked out and ferry service stopped. There were talks, rotating walkouts and eventually, on September 20, Bennett and the unions worked out a complex deal that sent everyone back to work. By that time the unemployment rate in B.C. was 14 per cent.

Olive branch bearers who negotiated the end of the Bill Bennett—Solidarity struggle: International Woodworkers of America (IWA) leader Jack Munro (above) and the premier's chief aide and adviser, Norman Spector (below).

Bennett won his third election victory in May 1983 and decided to start an even tougher restraint package. The NDP was, in effect, leaderless, as Barrett had lost interest and Bob Skelly did not take over as party leader for a year.

In two budgets and 40 separate bills, Bennett's government launched an onslaught on government expenditures and institutions and cut civil servant jobs. On July 27, about 20,000 people demonstrated outside the Legislature. Guards were posted outside the building and Bennett had a bodyguard. Labour had to provide the political opposition and Operation Solidarity, involving many B.C. unions, was formed. A general strike was set for October 31 and between 50 and 60 thousand people joined in a march past the Hotel Vancouver on October 15. The Socreds were inside at their annual convention.

Soon afterwards, olive branches became fashionable, and Jack Munro, the International Woodworkers of America leader, met Bennett and his chief adviser Norman Spector at Bennett's home in Kelowna. The strike threat was withdrawn and Bennett offered to reconsider some of the measures and to consult with union leaders on the restraint program. The collapse of Solidarity left bitter tastes in many union mouths. Bennett did little better. In December, a poll showed that 60 per cent were dissatisfied with the Bennett's restraint program and 30 per cent

Bill Vander Zalm has to beat off a strong slate in the Socred leadership race at Whistler in July 1986. Bud Smith, who headed Premier Bill Bennett's office, and Grace McCarthy, whose Socred services lasted more than 20 years, drop out in the early ballots. Now the fourth ballot is over and Attorney-General Brian Smith has lost to Vander Zalm. The rivals become friends, for a moment.

satisfied. The resentments and disappointment continued and, although Bennett could tell his cheering convention supporters in October 1985 that restraint had worked and that now civil servants jobs were safe, he decided to quit politics on May 22, 1986.

Of all the candidates to succeed Bennett, only four had a reasonable chance—Cabinet ministers Grace McCarthy, Brian Smith and Bud Smith, and Bill Vander Zalm. Unabashed by his failure to take the Vancouver mayor's seat away from docile, dogged Mike Harcourt in 1974, Vander Zalm campaigned for the premier's office with his usual effervescence and charm. He appeared to be well ahead before the leadership convention opened at Whistler in July. At the convention he led all the ballots and was sitting at his desk in the premier's office in Victoria on August 6, 1986. He then went on to beat the NDP's fumbling Bob Skelly (who had succeeded Dave Barrett in May 1984) and

Socred allies: Rita Johnston—premier between Bill Vander Zalm's resignation and the election defeat in 1991, Bill Reid—the former auto dealer who resigned from cabinet in a lottery money scandal, and Bill Vander Zalm celebrate victory in the battle for Surrey's leadership delegates in the summer of 1986.

won the October election by 47 seats to 22. No other party elected a member.

The next five years were, in essence, an exercise in the politics of absurdity. Scandal, arrogance and deceit covered the operations of government with a sheet of dishonour. Cabinet, caucus, senior bureaucrats and party officials—who normally provide the checks and balances to a wayward political leader—seemed unwilling or unable to act. The NDP, again, was paralysed by another search for a leader. Bob Skelly had quit as leader in November 1986, soon after the election. No-one of note seemed eager to take over, and Mike Harcourt got the job the next April; it took him several months to organise his demoralised party. As a result, the opposition to Vander Zalm came from the media and from party grassroots.

Bill Vander Zalm was forced to resign on April 2, 1991, when Conflict of Interest Commissioner Ted Hughes issued his report on the premier's $14,500,000 sale of his Fantasy Gardens theme park in Richmond. His political ally from Surrey, Rita Johnston, took over as interim premier. She won the Social Credit leadership race on July 21 and became premier. In the election on October 17, the Social Credit party was cut to seven seats and the Liberals, under Gordon Wilson, became the opposition. Mike Harcourt spent his first day as premier with an NDP government in Victoria on November 5, 1991.

From the early sixties, while the politicians and their friends in business, the unions and media squabbled and diminished the art of politics in British Columbia, another powerful force was mounting a challenge. Lobbies, pressure groups, single issue coalitions—whatever you might call them—grew during this period, especially during the 1970s. They ranged from large groups seeking more power and fair treatment

A logging truck leaves Carmanah Valley on Vancouver Island. The valley, and its stand of more than 200 rare, giant Sitka spruce, has become a symbol of the environmental conflict in B.C. politics.

One the one hand, conservationists maintain that the forest companies are stripping B.C.'s valleys and hillsides—economically and aesthetically. Sometimes by their side are the native people of the area who have endowed certain regions (such as the Carmanah) with spiritual and historical significance.

On the other side are the forest companies who maintain that they are obeying provincial laws, agreements and guidelines and need the timber to stay in business, employ workers and pay fees and taxes. By their side are the unions whose members have already lost thousands of jobs—and seem destined to lose more.

In the middle is the government. Even the free-enterprise Socreds soon realised that they could not ignore the conservationist movement. The NDP, both in opposition and in government, have been split between those who value union support and those who agree with the conservationists. The complicating factor for the B.C. government: how can it ensure that conservation and economic growth are allies, not deadly rivals?

for women, native peoples and other disadvantaged groups, those fighting for the protection of the environment to, say, a handful of people trying to save the few remaining members of an endangered species. Their sense ran from the profound to the weird. This is not the place to examine the growth and power of these groups—a subject neglected by both authors and journalists who focus on the immediate, not the long-term. But there's little denying that these groups have moved into the partial vacuum caused by political impotence, stupidity and wrong-doing.

Michael Harcourt had beat off a challenge from Bill Vander Zalm for the mayoralty of Vancouver in 1984. But no-one challenged him when he sought the leadership of the provincial NDP party, and he led the party to victory in 1991.

The causes espoused by these groups have been mostly national in scope. But the ministers in Victoria, instead of having to listen only to business, labour and the voters every four or five years, have had to enact new laws and regulations and make appointments that respond to the pressures of these groups. The environmental movement—through a mix of lobbying, propaganda and sometimes violent protests—has forced government, business and labour to regard the environment as a resource for all people instead of a cornucopia of taxes, cash and jobs. Women's groups forced changes that have transformed women's opportunities in the home, workplace and politics. Native people are now a powerful political force and have demanded, and won, recognition as a partner in the Confederation debate as well as the right to bargain on equal terms for their historic land and privileges.

These triumphs do not mean that the battles have been won, of course. But they do show that these struggles for the environment, women's rights and native peoples' rightful place in society have changed life in British Columbia just as dramatically, and perhaps more significantly, than have the acts of the political circus.

A Greek Restaurant on West Broadway, Vancouver

April 3, 1992

Upstairs in a small cubby-hole around a square table three men are sitting, sipping retsina and waiting for salad and calamari.

"Bit beneath you, this," says one of the men who is in his late forties, conservatively dressed—could be a loans officer in a downtown bank. That description would also suit the second man, but not the third. His curriculum vitae might consist of jobs in consulting firms that advise distraught personnel officers how to fire workers in a quick, bloodless, no-quarters coup.

"I thought we'd be out of the way here," said the third man. "No use attracting attention. None of us is exactly a Molson Three-Star Selection these days."

They were friends before becoming rivals for the Socred leadership in 1991: Rita Johnston (left) strides out of the Legislature with Grace McCarthy.

They start to eat.

"I brought these along."

The first man has three brown paper bags with eyeholes cut in them. He hands them round. They laugh awkwardly and stuff them on their chairs.

"What's the occasion? April Fool's Day was two days ago,?" asks the second man.

"It's the founding meeting of the S.C.S.C.—the Socred Campaign Survivors' Club. I think we should meet every April 3 in future. That's the day that Rita Johnston took over as interim premier from Vander Zalm. When the campaign really began."

They are quiet. The third man spits out his olive pit.

"What a change. We swapped Vander Zalm the gardener for Johnston the trailer-court lady. What a woman to make premier! That 'has someone peed in your Wheaties?' remark may have gone down well at a Whalley Ratepayers Social, but I often wonder if Robert Bourassa or Bob Rae would appreciate its subtlety."

These men are talking about the man and woman who have paid their wages for the past few years. They have obviously not bought their loyalty. These men are members of a select group which advises politicians and runs election campaigns. It does not seem to matter if their employers lose. If that happens, our friends here just get other jobs advising businessmen with, one hopes, better success.

"It was a classic case of failure, wasn't it." says the second man. "The campaign will probably be cited in textbooks as a case study in futility. The tour, for example. Poor Rita ended up at the end of the day in some plant up in the boonies—of interest to nobody. How could we get any TV time for her? Of course, you couldn't get time for her if you got her to...No, I shouldn't say it. She was a sincere woman who was wildly out of her depth. But those ads about the NDP in Ontario! And that half-hearted law-and-order campaign!"

He paused, but no-one else spoke.

"I think the last chance to save it rested with those delegate clowns. They had a chance to pick Grace McCarthy. After all, Rita had done nothing in her days as premier to show she could hold a candle to Mrs. McC."

The three men started to tackle the calamari. That made them thirsty and, after some wine, the conversation started to quicken. They agreed that Mrs. McCarthy was not their favourite sixty-year-old. She was, however, and they agreed on this, a first-rate political operator—something they could appreciate. They all said, between mouthfuls of squid and wine, that she had the courage and good sense to quit Cabinet on July 5, 1988 over the Expo Land/Peter Toigo/Peter Brown/Jack Poole/Li Ka Shing affair. She had also tried to get the premier to fire David Poole.

"Yes," said the second man, "I think she had distanced herself from Vander Zalm. We could have run a campaign with her that was full of renewal, a clean sweep—that kind of stuff. Mrs. Johnston had been tied up with the premier and Bill Reid for nearly 20 years."

"True. But I wonder," said the saturnine third man, "if there really was a chance of winning with anybody. I think poor Bill Bennett had done his best with B.C. Place, Expo, restraint—funny how it's back in fashion now with Mikey playing the hardnose—and he quit in '86 when he saw that the numbers were against him. I remember noticing how Bennett was horrified at Whistler when he saw that Vander Zalm led on all the ballots. After all, Bill remembered when Vander Zalm had his fun and games in Surrey. When he was in Bill's Cabinet he spoiled all the good policy plans with his threats and fibs and backtracking."

After the coffee had come and the plates were taken away, the three reminisced about Vander Zalm's election victory over NDP leader Robert Skelly in October, 1986.

"We should have been scared then," the first man murmured, "Poor Skelly was so terrible that there were tales that some of the caucus tried to kick him out a couple of weeks before the election! And Vander Zalm was miles ahead in the numbers game when the writ was dropped. Yet on October 22, we hadn't increased our popular vote and the NDP had only dropped two points."

And Vander Zalm, the premier?

The three agreed that from November 6, 1986, things went none too smoothly. The premier's office under David Poole was a mess and Vander Zalm showed that he was ready to go off half-cocked on almost anything—from abortion to the civil service.

"It seemed to me then—and I think it's still true—that Vander Zalm was unlike any other premier we've had."

The second man, quieter and more thoughtful than his friends, was talking. The Bennetts, and even Dave Barrett, he maintained, tried to do things they believed were good for the province, the party—and the friends who had helped them get there. But Vander Zalm spent most of his time as premier trying to get revenge on the people who had hurt him in the past—or people he didn't like.

Premier Vander Zalm learns of the perils caused when a premier conducts a business open to the public. Demonstrators at Fantasy Gardens berate the captive premier.

"It was essentially a personal vendetta. And some of the other things he tried to do—privatisation, decentralisation, Bill 19, tighter control over education and the banning of provincially-funded abortions—turned out disasters because his objective was revenge, not reform. There was virtually no consultation, no research, no political preparation. Unlike Bennett, he wanted to be a one-man show; he didn't involve the Cabinet and caucus and they were often more upset than the Opposition.

"Policy was not what was good for the province and the Social Credit party. It was what made Bill Vander Zalm happy.

"The potential for disaster in his holding onto Fantasy Gardens, despite all the advice about the risks of his being in conflict of interest, hovered over his head like a stormcloud. I certainly wasn't surprised when Ted Hughes' report forced him to quit or even when he was charged. Fancy a premier getting all tied up with someone like Faye Leung and writing financial agreements on hotel notepaper in the middle of the night for mysterious financiers from Hong Kong!"

They agreed—they did not botch the 1991 election campaign; it was lost years ago. The third man, the saturnine one, said:

"Same time, next year?"

Dates to Remember

11,000 years ago:	Hunters in Interior B.C.
9,000 years ago:	Native people on coast.
1774:	First Spanish exploration.
1778:	Captain Cook arrives at Nootka.
1789:	Spanish arrive at Nootka.
1792:	Captain Vancouver starts mapping coast.
1793:	Mackenzie reaches Pacific at Bella Coola.
1808:	Fraser reaches Pacific.
1827:	Fort Langley built.
1843:	Fort Victoria built.
1846:	Borders with U.S. fixed at 49th Parallel.
1849:	Vancouver Island created a crown colony.
1858:	Fraser gold rush begins.
1858:	New Caledonia becomes British Columbia.
1866:	Colonies of Vancouver Island and B.C. unite.
1867:	Confederation of Canada formed.
1871:	Terms of Union with Canada approved.
1880:	Work on B.C. section of CPR begins.
1885:	Last Spike driven home at Craigellachie.
1886:	City of Vancouver incorporated; burns down two months later.
1898:	Yukon Gold Rush.
1903:	Richard McBride named premier; party politics begin.
1914:	War with Germany.
1918:	CPR's Princess Sophia sinks; 346 die.
1929:	Jobless besiege Vancouver relief office.
1938:	Jobless take over Vancouver Post Office, Hotel Georgia, Art Gallery.
1939:	War with Germany.
1941:	Liberal-Conservative Coalition formed.
1952:	W.A.C. Bennett wins election.
1953:	Massive highway building program starts.
1967:	Duncan Dam on Columbia built.
1972:	NDP's Dave Barrett wins election.
1975:	Bill Bennett leads Socreds back to power.
1982:	Restraint program starts.
1986:	Bennett resigns; Bill Vander Zalm takes over.
1991:	Vander Zalm resigns; Rita Johnston takes over.
1991:	Mike Harcourt wins election for NDP.
1992:	New restraint program starts.

Books about British Columbia

Akrigg, G.P.V. and Helen Akrigg. *British Columbia Chronicle, 1778-1846 and 1847-1871.* 2 volumes. Vancouver: Discovery Press 1977.

Barman, Jean. *The West Beyond the West: A History of British Columbia.* Toronto: University of Toronto 1991

Berton, Pierre. *The Last Spike: The Great Railway 1881-1885.* Toronto: McClelland & Stewart 1971.

— *The Great Depression 1929-1939.* Toronto: McClelland & Stewart 1990

Brody, Hugh. *Maps and Dreams: Indians and the British Columbia Frontier.* Vancouver: Douglas & McIntyre 1981.

Fisher, Robin. *Contact and Conflict: Indian-European Relations in British Columbia.* Vancouver: UBC Press 1977.

— *Duff Pattullo.* Toronto 1991.

Fladmark, Knut. *British Columbia Prehistory.* Ottawa: National Museum of Man 1986.

Leslie, Graham. *Breach of Promise.* Madeira Park: Harbour 1990.

Mason, Gary and Keith Baldrey. *Fantasyland.* Toronto 1989.

Mitchell, David. *Succession: The Political Reshaping of British Columbia.* Vancouver: Douglas & McIntyre 1987.

— *W.A.C.: Bennett and the Rise of British Columbia.* Vancouver: Douglas & McIntyre 1983.

Persky, Stan. *Son of Socred.* Vancouver: New Star 1979.

— *Bennett II.* Vancouver: New Star 1987.

— *Fantasy Government: Bill Vander Zalm and the Future of Social Credit.* Vancouver: New Star 1989.

Robin, Martin. *The Rush For Spoils: The Company Province 1871-1933.* Toronto: McClelland & Stewart 1972.

— *Pillars of Profit: The Company Province 1934-1972.* Toronto: McClelland & Stewart 1973.

Sherman, Paddy. *Bennett.* Toronto 1963.

Twigg, Alan. *Vander Zalm: From Immigrant to Premier.* Madeira Park: Harbour 1986.

White, Howard. *Raincoast Chronicles.* Madeira Park: Harbour 1972.

Woodcock, George. *British Columbia, A History of the Province.* Vancouver: Douglas & McIntyre 1990.

Index

Many people helped to produce this book. Here are some of them:

Kevin Williams
The staff of the :
British Columbia Archives and Records Service
Vancouver Public Library.
Vancouver City Archives.
University of B.C. Special Collections.
Fraser Valley College.
British Columbia Hydro
British Columbia Ferry Corporation
Mining Asociation of British Columbia
British Columbia Ministry of Tourism

Photo Credits:

BCARS = British Columbia Archives and Record Service
CM = Cumberland Museum
MM = Maritime Museum of British Columbia, Victoria
PBC = Province of British Columbia
PP = Pacific Press Library
SFU = Simon Fraser University Archives
UBC = University of British Columbia Special Collections
VCA = Vancouver City Archives
VPL = Vancouver Public Library

Front Cover (clockwise)

Family and cabin in Interior, 190?—VPL 78366; Loggers and donkey engine at Pitt Lake, 1866—VPL 5590; Native women at Imperial Cannery in Steveston,1913—VPL 2111; New Parliament Buildings in Victoria,1900—CVA OUT-P.469, N.935; *Skuzzy* on the Fraser River, *1881*—VPL 698.

Chapter One

p.12—BCARS A-2678; p.15—BCARS PDP 2252; p.16—MM P-473; p.17—BCARS A-2312; p.18—CVA BO-P.1, N.3; p.19—BCARS A-1227; p.20—BCARS G-3584.

Chapter Two

p.28 (top)—CVA OUT-P.520, N.201; p.28 (bottom)—BCARS CM/A-78; p.29—BCARS A-8953; p.30—BCARS A-1722; p.31—BCARS C-6124; p.32—VPL 9195; p.34 (top)—BCARS A-3081; p.35—BCARS G-5497; p.36—BCARS A-1514; p.38—BCARS B-2767.

Chapter Three

p.44—VPL 2262; p.46—BCARS A-2037; p.47 (top)—CVA OUT-P.959, N.511; p.47 (bottom)—UBC; p.48—VPL 8690; p.49 (top)—VPL 19928; p.49 (bottom)—CVA IN-P.87, N.158; p.50 (top)—BCARS D-7548; p.50 (bottom)—VPL 7779; p.52—CVA CAN-P.2, N.56; p.53—CVA WAT-P.3, N.10; p.54—CVA 3-4 (F. Dally); p.55—VPL 78366; p.57—VPL 2134.

Chapter Four

p.60—CVA CAN-P.218, N.224; p. 61 (top)—BCARS D-6674; p.61 (bottom)—BCARS A-1321; p.62—VPL 391; p.64—VPL 698; p.65 (bottom)—CVA BO-P.55, N.14; p.65 (top)—VPL 6570; p.66—VPL 13246; p.67—VPL 2249; p.68—BCARS A-4407; p.69 (top)—VPL 5590; p.69 (bottom)—BCARS E-5059; p.70—CVA 260-1027 (James Crookall); p.71—VPL 19880-A; p.72—CVA BO-P.93, N.374#1; p.73—CVA BO-P.154, N.44; p.74—CVA PORT-P.543.

Chapter Five

p.76—CVA STR-P.336, N.307; p.77 (top)—VPL 509; p.77 (bottom)—VPL 27807; p.78 (top)—VPL 64047; p.79—CVA 196-1; p.80—VPL 1785; p.82—CM C-100.2; p.84—CVA PORT-P.817; p.85 (top)—CVA 371-119; p.85 (bottom)—VPL 11023; p.87 (bottom)— VPL 1786; p.88 (top)—CVA BU-P.403, N.387; p.88 (bottom)—VPL 9865; p.89—VPL 136; p.89 ; p.90 (top)—VPL 2639; p.90 (bottom)—VPL 2022; p.91 (top)—UBC; p.91 (bottom)—VPL 1380; p.92—VPL 13338; p.93—VPL 3038; p.95—VPL 1277; p.101 (top)—CVA OUT-P.1027, N.935; p.101 (bottom)—CVA OUT-P.469, N.935.

Chapter Six

p.104—BCARS H-5390; p.105—BCARS F-5599; p.107 (bottom)—PBC; p.107 (top)—BCARS H-5389; p.108 (top)—BCARS E-6844; p.108 (bottom)—BCARS H-5391; p.109 (top)—SFU; p.109 (bottom)—UBC; p.111—PP; p.112—BCARS H-5392; p.114—BCARS H-5393; p.115 (top)—PBC 16-02250; p.115 (bottom)—PBC 16-00200; p.117—PP; p.118 (top)—PP; p.118 (bottom)—PP; p.119 (top)—PP; p.119 (bottom)—PP; p.120—PP; p.121—PBC; p.123—PP; p.125—PP.

Printed in Canada